For the
Love
of
Life on Earth

For the

Love

of

Life on Earth

Liane Rich

The information contained in this book is not intended as a substitute for professional advice. Neither the publisher nor the author is engaged in rendering professional advice to the reader. The intent of the author is only to offer information of a general nature to assist you in your quest for emotional and spiritual well-being. In the event you use any of the information in this book for yourself, the author and the publisher assume no responsibility for your actions.

Loving Light Books
Copyright © 2017 Liane Rich

All rights reserved. This book may not be copied or reproduced in whole or in part, or transmitted in any form whatsoever, without written permission from the publisher, except for brief passages for review purposes.

ISBN 13: 978-1-878480-33-0
ISBN 10: 1-878480-33-2

Loving Light Books
www.lovinglightbooks.com
Also Available at:
Amazon: www.amazon.com
Barnes & Noble: www.barnesandnoble.com

Change how you see it!

According to quantum physics, "Your observation of an event changes the event."

Perception is everything....

Become the "observer" and you become the creator... of a whole new way of living this life on earth. See a good outcome in absolutely everything!

*for my friend E.T.,
a master at unconditional giving....*

"In this book I would like to help those of you who are ready, to learn more about what really happens when you die. You do not really go off to some far away place in the sky. You actually go "within" to the universe that is right inside of you. Keep in mind that all reality is already in place; and everything that is, or could possibly be, has already been created. You are a traveler and you are traveling through the vastness that is your own self.

This book is a gift to Liane. It is going to be very personal and it is meant to guide her in her next phase of this journey. If she chooses to publish this and if you choose to join us on this little journey, you will be most enlightened."

God

Preface

I recently saw an interview with songwriter/singer John Mellencamp. During this interview he was asked how he could write so many songs. He said, "Well, you have to be available." When the interviewer asked what he meant by "be available," Mellencamp replied, "When it comes through – you have to let it." He went on to say that he has written songs before and when finished he just looks up (he looked up to the ceiling in the interview) and says, "Thank you!"

The interviewer asked how many songs he wrote that way and he shook his head and said, "Oh – many, many songs."

This is how I feel about channeling these books. I have written many books by simply "being available."

This book was a little different. At first God tried to get me out of bed early one morning by saying, "I want to write now," and I just rolled over, pulled the cover over my head, smiled and said, "No you don't!"

I really did think he was just kidding, because I

felt like I had just finished publishing our last book *Your Individual Divinity: Existing in Parallel Realities*. I felt like I needed more time off.

Later that day, I sat down to ask God a question. That's when God took over and started his new book. The question I asked had to do with near-death experiences. In the past several months I had been drawn to books relating to NDEs, and I found it interesting that each individual seems to experience the After Life through a filter of their own background or beliefs. The following is the answer I received to my question regarding this. I always begin my writings with, "God – are you light?"

Liane: God – are you light?
God: Yes.
Liane: I don't understand the NDE? Why are they so different?
God: Each individual sees what they are meant to see for their own well-being. It is as though the floodgates of their consciousness "open" and they begin to see what is laying dormant in their consciousness. They do not see what they "wish" to see so much as they see what is stored "in" them.
Liane: So they haven't really died and gone somewhere?
God: No! There is nowhere to go. You do not leave your body and go out into the ethers when you

die. You do go "within," which is where absolutely everything exists. Consciousness is an inside job. You live in your consciousness and it is made up of all that you are and all that you have ever been and all that you will be. Your consciousness does not leave you and "all" dimensions are "within" you. You are a multi-dimensional being and you "exist" on many dimensions at one time.

All time is simultaneous and is occurring right now this moment. When the brain dies, it "allows" your consciousness to come forward and open up to greater possibilities. This is due to the fact that you live in a limited human body with a limited human brain. When you are what you call dead, your brain is relaxed and no longer sending the signals that keep all the gates closed to new possibilities. The gates are released and everything is set free including consciousness.

Most people like to confine consciousness and control consciousness to some degree. In death your consciousness is actually set free and you become more "real" than your earthly consciousness. You become more aware and more expanded. A child's "view" or "perception" of reality is made up of all that the child has been exposed to thus far. This includes exposure while in the womb. An adult has a greater awareness of how to operate and manipulate this material plane by his or her length of experience here and how aware he or she may have been.

When any adult dies or leaves his or her body, they do so in an effort to continue on. The soul does not go out into the ethers somewhere. The soul turns "within" to its source. It begins to move in an inward direction within the nucleus of its own self. Think of each individual as a cell within the body of God. In the same way that the cells within your body die off or grow, you will die off or grow within the body of God. If you decide to go another round you will multiply and create more cells. You call these cells your offspring.

So, as you die you actually dissolve into the body of God that you exist in. You are **not** separate from the main body of God and you do not leave the main body… not ever!

(The writing stops)
Liane: God, are you finished?
God: Yes!

(But I wanted more….)
Liane: God, tell me more please.
God: You will begin to understand the workings of human consciousness by looking at how you create. You are a creative being and you are creating right now this instant. You send out signals and energy that literally affect what you see and how you see it. You use your personal interpretation of

something to "allow" that something to become what you wish it to be. In the same way that you project your thoughts out to form an opinion, you also project your energy into your thoughts to create the type of world you live in.

Now, since we all know how we are creative beings who are part of a divine creative force, it is no surprise that we would continue on and never really ever end. You are from God and you are made up of God energy. Since no energy is ever separate, you are never separate from God.

If you decide to die, you simply "change" your energy. Since you are in a human body, made partly of mass, you would tend to remove your consciousness from that body and look around you. Your consciousness is aware on certain levels of much more than your puny little mind and your limited thoughts.

I don't want to upset you, but you are quite limited in your human form. You are dumbed-down from all that you truly are, in order to play this game that we will call "Life on Earth."

So, since you are dumbed-down you will find it quite extraordinary to know that you are actually a divine creative force. You project out the world that you see and you even change the world that you see by how you judge it or name it. You continue to be a divine creative force when you die. This is due to the fact that you never really die or, better said, you never

ever end.

So, if the divine creator in you continues on, don't you think that you create your own life after life? Don't you think that you would continue to project out image after image from all the creative energy that is stored in your consciousness? Think about it! You are everything and you contain everything! You are a piece of God! You are a cell within the body of God! Do you think it is so difficult for you to project a beautiful scene when your brain shuts off? Your brain limits you in many ways. Why would you want to "believe" that when your brain is gone, you are gone?

So, as you can see we have a great deal to discuss in this new book in our Loving Light Books. Let's get to it….

(I still didn't feel like my body was ready to channel a new book and so God said to me)

God: You are ready. We* are ready. Get out of our way and let us do our work.

Liane: I'll do my best ♥. Do you have a title picked out?

God: Yes – it is, *For the Love of Life on Earth.*

* It's explained in the first book that these books are being written for you by God and all of our souls.

Note from Liane

For those of you who are new to God's books and curious to know more about the source of this information, I have published a small book titled, *For the Love of God: An Introduction to God*. This small book will give you a great deal of insight into this voice that speaks to me and writes through me. *For the Love of God: An Introduction to God* also appears as the Introduction to our book titled, *The Book of Love*. Either book will give you greater insight into this voice and the source of this information.

In the back of this book you will find a brief description of my first encounter with the God voice as well as a full list of book titles. I am told that repetition is used as a teaching tool in these books. God uses repetition freely and says that's the fastest way to get through our judgmental, conscious mind to the subconscious.

I hand write (channel) each book and type them myself. There is no editing of this material, so you are reading the original version as it was channeled by me. I think of this information as God giving me my own personal answers and guiding me to a more fulfilling life.

I hope you enjoy the insights presented here and that they may help you to have a happier, healthier and more peaceful life.

In loving light, *Liane*

*Y*ou will come to a place in your role as a human on earth that may be most fearful. This place is acceptance. Acceptance is most difficult for you as you do not understand your role as a human being. You see yourself as human and not so much as a being of light energy.

As you evolve as a human being you begin to take on more and more human traits and you begin to move away from your core which is that of a light being. The light being that resides within you does not experience life on earth in the same way that you (the human you) experience life on earth. The light being in you knows no wrong and sees no wrong, as it is from God. The light being in you is unafraid and knows only energy in movement. The light being in you does not judge how the energy of life on earth moves or where it goes. The light being in you simply *allows* for all areas of creation, simply because this light being has experienced all areas of creation and is well *aware* of the fact that creation is an illusion; it is a dream. If you are *dreaming* that you die, do you really die? If you are dreaming that ten thousand or ten million die, do they really die?

You live in a dream! You do not die ever! You go on and on and on forever! If you can get this part straight in your head, you will be light years ahead of this game that we will call "Coming to Earth to Experience a Vivid Dream." In the same way that you lie down or go to bed and experience vivid dreams, you actually come here in droves to *experience* this giant dream of mass consciousness. You love to come for whatever reasons, and once you leave this realm you usually make up excuses as to why you must return. Some of you call it "karmic debt" while others simply call it "the game of life." Regardless of what you call it, you tend to return to this playground often.

Now, once you have returned, you no longer *remember* that you are this light being and you begin the struggle to find your way through the denser energies that surround this dimension. Once you get here you go completely unconscious of the fact that you are indeed a light being and you exist forever, and you actually may exist in more than one dimension at any given time.

So, as a light being, you begin to lose *your* consciousness and the human part begins to take over and your dream state begins. As you know, dreams can be fun and they can also be a little stressful. Your dream on earth will proceed according to your level of consciousness. In other words, the more of your light being you can connect with and stay connected to, the greater your chance of bringing light and consciousness into your dream. The dreamer is simply asleep and experiencing *imagination* which is creative energy. So you are basically *creating* your own personal dream out of your own personal imagination? And what is imagination? It is creative energy at work. Your imagination is creative energy making images within your consciousness so that you might enjoy life in this dimension. The greater your connection to, and with, the light being *in* you; the better your dream experience becomes.

It's all a game that you play with yourself. You wish to enjoy yourself and your imagination and so you literally adventure *into* your imagination which allows you to experience absolutely anything *you* choose to experience. On some level it is all you experiencing all that is in you, or your imagination.

So, as you experience and dream your way through this dimension or "this earth dream," I would like you to remember the most important part of your earth experience which is this: you do not end... not ever! Your neighbor does not end... not ever! Please come out of the denser energies of judgment and pain. You are bringing yourself down and you are bringing your dream down into the slower denser energies. If you can stay in the lighter, faster, higher energies of love and acceptance, your dream on earth will be much more pleasurable. Unconditional love is the most powerful energy here in this dream. *Unconditional* means just that – no conditions placed on your love. Love is acceptance of what is and love is sorely needed if you wish to keep your own personal dream from turning into a nightmare. Sweet dreams are more enjoyable and sweet dreams come from a sweet, joyful imagination. Dream well and dream of angels and light beings….

---

*Y*ou will begin to discover how you have entered a body in the hopes of experiencing life on planet earth. Some of you believe that you come here to experience joy and happiness while others believe that you come here to raise the vibration surrounding this dimension. Whatever your purpose for being here, you lose conscious awareness of your plans once you enter. For one thing, you enter into a fetus (or sometimes a small baby) in an effort to experience life on earth.

So, here we have this light being, who is quite capable of creating and is quite accomplished and "aware" on the spiritual planes, and he/she/it enters this earth plane and within a very short time is rendered unconscious. Why on earth do you suppose you chose to enter such a situation? Well, the answer to that is quite varied and quite personal to each individual light being. You may choose to come here for fun and games or you may choose to come here to add a little love and light. The reasons for coming here are as varied as the humans who are here.

Once you have entered this earth plane, you lose consciousness fairly soon after entering. This is due to the energy vibration that surrounds this dimension. You may begin your life on earth as a totally unconscious light being or you may retain some memory of your true identity for a brief time. You begin to fade quickly as you are *light* and you are now surrounded by the denser energies that tend to pull light down. Light vibrates quite fast, and to live on planet earth is like trying to run in quicksand. You may get pulled down (energy wise) into this slower, denser environment. You, however, are quite aware of this fact before you ever enter this dimension.

So, now we have you successfully *in* a human body or form and you know you came for a reason, however, you do not remember why you came. Have you ever gone into a room in your home and wondered what you came into that room for? Often you may start to do something and then think, "Wait, how was I going to do this?" It's like that. You came into this dimension but you do not remember why.

So, how do we get you to remember that you

are a light being and that you came here to affect change by raising the light vibration here? We get you to *realize* that you are more than just a human body. We remind you of all the miraculous and wonderful, magical qualities that you have inside of you. We remind you that you are loved and how you contain love. We reconnect you with your source. We plug you back into your source, which is the greatest light being of all. We reconnect you with "all that is" in an effort to kick-start your own personal light being within you.

We just have to remind you of who you really are and then guide you in that direction. This is what this "new age" is all about. It is about you waking up to your true identity so that *you* might become aware and conscious once again; and begin to vibrate much faster, so that *you* may rise above the denser energies that slow your vibration.

You can help. You can assist in this waking up process. Many of you have begun and are using your mind and your emotions to raise your level of vibration now. This is a time of great change and it is a time of waking up and rising up. You will begin to awaken to the fact that you are a light being and this will change everything!

As far as you can see from where you are, there is light. Light permeates this dimension and is alive and vivid. The problem is with your vision. You do not see the light that is all around you simply because you are not yet operating from a higher level.

What if I were to tell you that life on earth can be paradise divine? Would you believe me? I am sure there have been points in your life that you actually felt were heavenly and I am also certain that those brief moments vanished within a very short time. Heaven on earth is your goal if you came here to experience the light within the confines of this earthly, material plane. So, if you purposely entered earth to *enjoy* all that planet earth has to offer, don't you think you would enjoy it more if you stop judging it or seeing it as harmful, dangerous and painful? You determine how any instant is perceived by how you see it. Try not to see it as dark and try to see it as light.

You get to determine whether you see a dark, fear-filled day or a light, bright, love-filled day. You get to determine whether you bemoan your circumstances in life or whether you *accept* your circumstances in life on earth. You get to *choose* whether you see the good in any given situation or whether you see it as bad or dangerous. You may change how you see it by simply changing your mind. I will now give you an example: you have a friend who is very sick and dying. You become fearful regarding their health and well-being. You try to convince your friend to fight for his or her life and to do absolutely everything possible to stay alive and well and living.

Your friend does not listen to your concerns and your friend continues to do things that are not necessarily considered healthy and not so helpful to healing. You are becoming very upset with your friend and you try hard to influence them in the direction of healing and thriving. Your friend, however, does not seem to care and is unmotivated. You become sad and fearful that this person you love is going to die and so you push harder to get them to listen to you. Life becomes a struggle for your friend, you become angry and confused and frustrated with them for not following your helpful advice.

Have you ever thought about simply accepting death and dying in the same way that you accept it when your child moves out of your home to live on their own? Have you ever thought that death may be a huge gift to the one who is dying? Have you ever thought that death may be a doorway to a wonderful adventure for the light being that is inhabiting and now leaving the body? It is good to look at all possibilities and not get too caught up in the fear that surrounds you. You may choose to tune in to the love that surrounds you and then, and only then, will you see how beautiful life on earth really is.

Think about it! The majority of your concerns revolve around sickness and health. You may choose to *accept* sickness as a part of the journey or you may fight it with all your might. Acceptance allows you to own the experience and to accept any outcome. Fighting, or blocking the energy does not allow you to own it or to work with it and feel it.

Look, I know you do not want to hear this and Liane does not want to channel this information for you, but I have found it necessary to go deeper now; and to explain for those of you who are ready, how you may create a better existence for yourselves on planet earth. Going with the flow of energy until it changes direction on its own is a very good idea. Acceptance of life "just as it is" is a good idea. You can do no wrong here… everything is flexible, movable, changeable energy. Work with the energy and let go of the fight and the struggle to survive on earth.

Allow yourself and your friends to simply "be." Do not insist that anyone perform in a certain way just to make you feel happier. Live and let live. Let them die if they choose to do so.

It is really none of your business. You have judged death so harshly and it is your greatest fear on planet earth. This is why I am asking you to see it differently. Please come out of your fear of death and into an acceptance that absolutely everything is okay and well in God's reality. And here is a news flash –

absolutely everything is God's reality! Nothing is left out of God and there is absolutely nothing but God.

So, leave your vivid, fearful imagination behind and move into a state of love and acceptance. Nothing is wrong, nothing is bad, you can do no wrong and there is nothing to fear. Do not be so afraid of someone leaving earth and moving on to another beautiful experience within another dimension of God's created reality. God is vast indeed and you are all safe and loved beyond measure within this God force that contains absolutely everything.

Your friend is simply creating a way to move on to a new level in a new dimension. You are simply fighting and struggling to keep your friend here on earth. Allow every light being to walk their own path and move on when they wish to. It is all just life on earth and you (the light being in you) knew ahead of time about the challenges and even some of the situations you chose to experience before coming here.

This will do for now as I am taxing Liane by writing so freely about death….

※

*W*hen you begin to see death as part of living, you will become a little less afraid of death and you will feel less pain when someone dies. Death is not morbid and death can actually become something to celebrate. Think of it as the light being inside the human form being released to expand its consciousness once again.

Light is quite expansive in nature and light is quite high in vibration. In order for light to enter a body, that light must condense and lower its vibration. It is like squeezing into a bottle that this light being must learn to exist within. It is like losing consciousness and waking up in a bottle. Wouldn't you feel good if you could get out of your bottle? Wouldn't you feel good to expand your consciousness once again?

Now, don't get me wrong here. I am not saying that it's a punishment to come to earth and enter a body. I'm just letting you know that it is a challenge for a light being to regain full consciousness, or any consciousness, and exist within the confines of the human body. Look at me... I am within Liane's body and she at least has contact with me and allows me to interact with her and allows me to connect to the source and run information through her. You may not believe that this information comes from God, however, it is a direct result of a light being within a body sending information (which is energy) out of the body, down through the arm and hand and onto paper. Her arm will sometimes try to block information that is unacceptable to the body such as information regarding death.

There is so much fear around death that you on earth don't even know how to discuss it. This is why I am channeling this information to you even though you do not wish to hear about death or read about death. The bottom line is this: you cannot create heaven on earth if you continue to live in fear of death. So, I am writing this information in an effort to release your very real fears, in order to *allow* you to rise "up" a little higher in your vibration. Dense fear brings you "down." Even when you are not thinking about it, it is *in* you and it is affecting the level at which you operate.

Now, I do not expect a huge audience to read this information. I do expect those of you who are looking to rise up in awareness and to raise your vibration in doing so, to find this information helpful. I do not see everyone *accepting* this information. However, I do expect to assist the few who are ready to know more about how you *always* continue to exist and you never ever end.

So, as we continue to see how such a small thing as leaving one's body can be frightening to those left behind, we will continue to see how there really is nothing to fear… ever!

I want you to realize that nothing you do or can do is ever wrong! I want you to see how you enter this material plane to play and to act out roles. I want you to see how you are a visitor here and you do *not* really exist here. You are a projection of something much greater than your individual self. You are part of a giant force or source and you only *feel* separate.

Once you learn to separate your true self from the role that you are playing, you will begin to see how you are so much greater than you realize. You tend to take on a personality, and you then love or hate your personality depending on how you *feel* about your role in the scheme of things. I will tell you now that your role is that of a human experiencing a very dense world of matter. This human is often afraid and confused and feels inadequate. The more afraid and confused one feels, the greater the level of fear that arises from situations. The higher or greater your level of fear, the harder or more stressful life on earth feels.

The trick is to get you to fully realize that you are not bad nor are you sinners! You are simply exploring this dimension and playing the role of a human. Your role may be anything you choose and your role may be changed at any time. Remember – you are the light being inside the material form or body. Your body is your costume and you will remove this costume at some point and leave it behind as you return home to your source. However, there is another option. Those of you who are learning Ascension may well be aware of the fact that as you raise your level of awareness and consciousness, you literally raise your vibration or speed up the vibration of your human body. This shift "up" in vibration allows the human form to vibrate faster and faster until, eventually; the human form may match the vibration of the light being inside. When the vibration is high enough, the material form may turn to particles of light and begin to *merge* with the light being that occupies it.

This is one of the reasons you all enjoy this plane and you choose to enter life on earth. If a body matches the vibration of the light being inhabiting it, it may then take on the qualities of the light being. This allows both the body and the light being to travel freely to other planes of reality and to experience what I will call Ascension liftoff. You will begin to lift up off this earth and disappear into light particles as you do so. You will begin to appear and disappear at will. This is possible and has been accomplished by a few who have inhabited this material plane.

Remember, everything is energy and matter is no different. Matter is simply particles of light held down by a slow movement. Once you speed things up and vibrate very fast, they can literally disappear from human view. They may then move on or stay in this dimension and play in this dimension. Later, with a few adjustments, the body may reappear in a different location on planet earth. This is all possible and will be accomplished, or I should say has already been accomplished in your future.

You see, there really is no time and this accomplishment has already occurred many, many times in your future.

You are creative beings and you come from, or better put, you are extensions of the creative source or force that is usually referred to as God. You are capable of creating and shape-shifting and much, much more. You have the ability to rise up and transfer physical matter to the extent that you take it with you.

So, now you tell me, what is the difference between raising your vibration to achieve physical lift off to leave earth, and taking off the body or costume and leaving it behind? Each is simply a way of leaving life on earth and each is achievable and doable for all of you.

❀

The beginning of your problems concerning the fact that you are a creative force began simply because you are an unconscious human being. Once you become conscious of the fact that you are creative, you will begin to use your powers a little more carefully. You will begin to create answers and solutions where you now may be creating problems and confusion.

Once you become a conscious human being, you will let go of complaining and anger. You will automatically *feel* gratitude for absolutely every situation you encounter and you will *recognize* a gift in absolutely every situation. This will become your new norm and this will become a lot of fun for you.

When you become conscious, you no longer see life on earth as dangerous. You begin to see life on earth as a great big *gift* and not so much of a challenge. You will find yourself enjoying the fact that you create your life as you go, and you will enjoy the fact that *you* decided to come to earth for the adventure. Many of you do not seem to enjoy your time once you arrive, and this is directly related to the level of awareness you may or may not have achieved. Some of you will *decide* to leave earth and return to the source and this too is okay. Absolutely anything you choose to do is okay!

So, as you continue to live out your life on earth, you may wish to take a deep breath and relax and let go. Let go of criticizing and let go of judging. Do not focus on what you do not like, as you will cause yourself to move in the direction you are focused on. If you focus on things or situations that make you angry, you will begin to move toward them. If you focus on things or situations that make you happy, you will begin to move toward those. This is how creating works. You take part in your creation and you are the one pointing the way. Watch where you *focus,* or where you choose to go.

Now, there is also such a thing as co-creating. Many of you band together, and focusing on the same direction can affect the vibration and movement of the entire group. You also have the ability to co-create with your source or God force. You are part of this huge mass of energy consciousness that is never-ending and all expansive. This force may, from time to time, communicate with those who are open to such communication and this force may assist in your life on earth.

So, if you *decide* to connect and communicate with this part of yourself known here as the light being *in* you, you may do so to reconnect with your source. Once you achieve a conscious reconnection with your source, you may decide to *allow* source, or God force, to do the creating for you. This, of course, takes a bit of trust which is foreign to many of you. The lack of trust on earth is quite high, and it blocks the energy of trust from being used and held on to. I would say that you on earth do not really accept "trust in God your source" as a possibility. You are taught to rely on your own abilities and you are not taught to trust life or God.

So, we are starting at the bottom with you here. We are starting with mistrust, fear, lack of consciousness, and a loss of awareness of your true identity and your *connection* to God.

Your third way to create your life on earth is to turn the choices over to God and *allow* God to guide you into a brighter future. This has worked for some of you and yet you continue to not trust the gifts once you receive them. Your life on earth seems to be based on two things: "How far up the ladder of wealth can I climb?" and "How wrong or right – good or bad am I?" You do not seem to realize yet that you do choose to come here to play and enjoy and explore. You do not necessarily come to earth to suffer and to struggle.

It is time now to give up the constant struggle and to begin to float with your life. This will turn your life on earth into a more pleasurable experience. Once you begin to experience pleasure in place of pain of struggle, you will become a much more peaceful group of human beings. You may actually begin to *enjoy* not being in control of everything.

So, for today, I would like to invite you to "let go and float" through your day. Stop criticism and judgment and anger and sorrow and just float. Think of it as God holding you up in a stream of water. I will not drop you. You may feel some turbulence in the water, and water may splash over you. The thing to remember is that God is holding you up and you are safe!

---

*A*s you become aware of your entire beingness, you will begin to realize that you are more than simply your material form. You are filled with spirit or soul energy. You are comprised of huge amounts of vibrating energy that allows you to breathe in and breathe out.

You are so much more than your human form and it is time for you to begin to *merge* with the spirit or light being that is you. You have been disconnected from this most valuable part of you and now it is time to reconnect. If you can just begin to relate to yourself as more than a body to be pushed and pulled at to do more and be more, you will have done well.

You must learn to *accept* yourself as a spiritual being if you wish to use your power and creative force to your full potential. You are not so much disconnected from the light being *in* you as you are in denial of the fact that you are indeed a light being who chose to enter this life on earth and to have this experience. So, if you went to all the time and effort to find a fetus to enter or even a baby to enter, don't you think there may be a reason you came to earth?

Some of you believe that you have a life purpose and others do not. This is as it should be. Often a spirit will enter this plane in an effort to explore and simply enjoy the ride. It is like going to Disneyland. Some go for fun and some actually work there. Some go because they are invited by a friend to help in some way and some go because they are curious. Then we have those who are trying to make things right. Some of you got off track and forgot to have a good time and so you came back to do a better job. Whatever your reason for your life on earth, you are here now and you are unaware of why you came.

You may decide to reconnect with the spirit *in* you in order to learn who you really are and maybe even why you came to earth. Most of you think only in survival terms: how to stay afloat; how to get ahead financially; how to be successful and how to be accepted and loved. You are not accustomed to your role as spirit or light being and you do not know how to behave as a spirit or light being.

Most of you find it quite difficult to be free of mental worry and fear and mistrust. A spirit does not have these concerns, as spirit is aware on a whole different level. One of the gifts of reconnecting with the light being, or spirit *in* you, is that your life becomes less fearful. You will trust more, simply because you will be trusting the part of you that is directly connected to God force. You will be in a stream of energy that allows you to be free of some of the human confusion that surrounds you every day on earth. There is such a strong energy of fear that surrounds this planet that it is difficult to not be affected by it. This dense energy affects all who live on earth and is just now being recognized by some of you.

So, if you wish for help in dealing with some of this energy, you may want to reconnect now with the light being that is in you. This light is literally in every cell of your body and is constantly working behind the scenes to support you and lift you up. This light that is in every cell *in* you is always in you and always *aware* on a higher level. This awareness allows the light *in* you to assist you, by showing you possibilities and answers that are not often available to your fearful mind. This light that is higher in awareness is constantly working for you and assisting you in your life on earth. This light that is *in* you is for you and not against you. This light that is *in* you does not ask for anything from you, and only waits for you to wake up and realize that you contain a light being that is really in charge of this mission on earth. And just what is your mission on earth? You are here for various and uncountable reasons. You are here for all the reasons your spirit chose to come to earth.

So, if you wish to know more about you, I would highly suggest you begin to merge with or reconnect with the living, vibrating light in you! This will allow you to raise your vibration up from fear in a very big way. So, how do we connect with a light being? Your cells are always communicating with one another. Atoms communicate with one another. The tiniest particles of energy communicate with one another. Communication is constant in nature and in life on earth.

I suggest that you look down at your body or go to your mirror and look into your eyes. Say, "hello," to you. Communicate with your body and work *in* to your spirit. You may talk to your body and thank it for serving you today. Thank your heart for pumping blood to your veins and eyes and mind to allow you to read this book. Thank your legs for carrying you forward in your day. If you do not have legs that move, be thankful for having the mind to read this. After you become accustomed to thanking your body for all the wonderful things it does for you, begin to thank your spirit for supporting you by running light energy through your entire body. When spirit leaves a body it is gone and the body usually does not move. When a body is unconscious the spirit is actually out. This does occur in some cases and when spirit returns, the body once again becomes conscious. The spirit does not always return and the body may be kept alive in other ways. Life support is not always true life support.

Now, when you begin to communicate with spirit, keep it simple. No rituals are required unless *you* believe they are necessary. When I first communicated with Liane she was quite frightened. She had been communicating with what she believed to be a spirit guide for less than a year when I *decided* she was ready to do the work she came to earth to do. She was unaware of her purpose this lifetime and I did not push her to do this work. She originally began communicating with her soul/spirit by sitting down with a pencil and paper and writing, "Is anyone there?" She then placed the pencil lightly on her notepad and watched in amazement as a giant "YES" was spelled out. This was some 30 years ago and she has done well with her communication.

I have explained to Liane that the spirit guide she believed she spoke with and dearly loved was actually the soul in her which is directly connected to God force. Since she was so gullible it was easy for me to begin to communicate with her outright. By gullible I mean innocent and unsophisticated of mind. She allowed me to actually speak to her, and once she was over her initial fear of communicating with me we began to work on my books. The more I spoke to her and wrote through her, the stronger our communication became.

How strong? Well, I am capable of waking her from sound sleep and quietly telling her that I want to write. She has become very happy with our arrangement. I write the books and she sits up and holds the pen. If I can do as much with one of you, I can do as much with all of you. There are many now who are assisting the God force in this way and it all begins with open communication. Do not be afraid to communicate with your soul/spirit. Be unafraid of any part of you!

※

You will begin to understand more about being a light being as you continue to focus on this part of yourself. As you concentrate on the light that dwells within your cells, you will be allowing your consciousness to expand.

Expanded consciousness is what it's all about. The more expansive you become the greater your ability to rise up to the higher levels of awareness. Awareness depends on accessibility to information and energy. Awareness is a knowingness that comes from a higher vibration. When you connect to the higher vibrations, you gradually let go of your hold on the lower vibrations. The lower vibrations are just that –

low. You wish to raise yourself in vibration and achieve success by rising "up" in awareness. This rise "up" allows you to live in peace with the earth and with other humans. You will find that it is most difficult to harm anyone when you are in a high level of awareness.

When you achieve a rise in your level of awareness, you will begin to "feel" on a whole new level. This feeling experience will allow you to know how others feel and is an extreme form of empathy. Once empathy has come into your energy field, you will no longer be able to cause pain for another. With empathy at this level, you would literally "feel" any emotional or mental or even physical pain that you might subject others to. You will literally be hurting you by hurting them!

This is how you will know when you have truly risen in awareness. You will no longer be able to push at another human, or animal, in an aggressive manner. You will have "felt" how you are all one and all connected. You will not be kind and loving to them because you mentally "know" you are part of them, but because you "feel" how you are part of them.

Here is the interesting thing: once you "feel" your connection to others, you will not only feel more nurturing to them, you will feel more nurturing toward yourself! You will be loving you by loving all!

So, as you continue to raise your level of

awareness, you will be healing you and them and this planet that you have chosen to visit. You are a guest here and you are unaware of the fact that you are. You are just passing through on your journey and you are so unconscious and unaware, that you act like you own this planet and you do not. You act like you own people and you do not. You are not in charge of them, nor are you in charge of this solar system, nor are you in charge of this universe. You are a visitor here; no more, no less.

I expect you to behave as a visitor would behave, and to be polite and to be peaceful and respectful to the others who are visiting. Do not use your creative abilities to cause harm. Use your creative abilities to raise yourself up to the higher vibrations that are available to you. You will find that you will be raising them up a notch by raising you up a notch.

This three-dimensional world is set up in such a way that you are not always seeing what is real. You are often seeing an illusion that is being projected by you and through you, and is coming from a belief that you have stored "in you." Let go of any low-level beliefs that may cause you problems. Low level beliefs bring you down and are usually associated with some sort of fear, which can quickly turn to frustration and then anger. Let these low level beliefs and ideas go! When you have an idea or thought that is less than uplifting for you or for someone else, please let it go and do not expand on this type of idea.

Ideas and thoughts of putting someone else down only succeed in putting *you* down in some way. You may go down emotionally and no longer feel happy, or you may go down physically by falling or bumping into something. You may even go down financially or you may simply take something away from yourself by losing it. Why? Simply because you want someone else to lose, and by doing so you are sending energy signals through your body which seek revenge. Revenge on someone else is really revenge on you, simply because this down-putting energy is now running through your body.

Please be polite and respectful while visiting earth. You are a light being living in a human body and you have forgotten that you are part of God. God creates! God has creative abilities and the light that resides "in" you is at your disposal. You control the light that is in you simply because this light that is energy can not experience this earth plane without a body. The senses are contained within the body. Light that comes to earth quickly dissipates into the ethers if it is in energy form. Light that comes to this earth in a body is allowed to grow and to expand; and in doing so, to lift this body up and to lift this planet up.

You are all here to lift yourself "up" not to put yourself "down." You will get this eventually and once you get the hang of being a creative light being in a human body, you will do wondrous and glorious things with your newfound awareness of self. Please focus "within" as the outside is simply a reflection of all that you are projecting at this time. If it is not "in you," you will not see it in your outside world. Perception is everything and everything really is well....

⁂

*Y*ou will continue to raise your vibration until you have reached a melding point. This melding point is where you become *aware* that you are God and God is you. You will come to this melding point by allowing yourself to continue to rise up. You allow yourself to continue to rise up by letting, or allowing, yourself to explore your inner realms.

Your inner realms are the part of you that you are the least aware of. You focus most of your attention on your outer self and the world around you. By going within yourself you begin to focus on what is contained inside of your body. You not only contain organs and blood vessels and nerves and cells, you also contain vast stores of information in the form of beliefs and thoughts and imagined harmful ideas, and even a few magical thoughts and ideas.

Most of your thoughts and ideas have been

with you for more than just this lifetime. Most of your thoughts and ideas have been influencing you for a very long time. The trick to rising "up" is in "letting go." Let go of old baggage. Allow yourself to rise by allowing yourself to lose some of the denser fear energy that holds you down. Allow the light in you to lift you higher by setting it free to guide you. Once you allow your light being to begin to expand, it will take over and assist you in this three-dimensional world.

You all have this light being inside of you and you are unaware of its presence. Some of you refer to having a spirit or soul within, however, you do not think much about it and many of you, actually most of you, would never think of communicating with this most valuable higher part of your own self. You sit in your worry and your fear and your problems and you feel so alone when, in actuality, you have a guide; a friend; a highly aware part of you that can become a part of your life if you simply *allow* it to.

You all have this light "in" you! You are all from the creative force that you call God. You have a soul! You are a soul! You are a spirit who came to this three-dimensional world and entered a body. In some cases you entered more than one body. In some cases, you split your energy field and you entered more than one body. Now, if a spirit, an energy force, has the wherewithal to enter this three-dimensional world at will and to then inseminate itself into a fetus or a body, don't you think it is quite evolved and maybe has intelligence? Wouldn't you want to get to "know" this particular entity, or light force, if you could?

Here's the truth of it – you can! You can get to know God by accepting the part of you that has come directly from God. You may choose to communicate directly with God or you may choose to communicate with your own soul/spirit/light. It is all up to you. You have this amazing part of you and you think you are so boring, or even unacceptable. Maybe, just maybe, you will begin to form a bond with this God-in-you part of you, and in doing so; you will begin a very beautiful, loving, kind relationship that is truly remarkable.

Speak with your soul. You will find your relationship with you to be the most remarkable relationship you will have on this planet. My first book that I asked Liane to write is titled, *God Spoke through Me to Tell You to Speak to Him.* I did not have the ability at that time to converse with Liane on many issues as she contained a great deal of fear regarding God and judgment day. Her fears and beliefs sometimes got in the way, but as you can see we make a great team and she is much better at allowing God to guide her life.

As you grow out of your fear of not being in control all the time, you too will relax and begin to trust God. God does not receive much trust these days and this too will change as you continue to raise your awareness. You must begin to trust God, as God is who you truly are. You contain God and God contains you. You are part of God force and you think you are simply a human who is trying to survive in this three-dimensional world. You are so much more than human. You are God! You are light! You are a creative light being and with a little guidance you will begin to calm down enough that you will be unafraid of "going with the flow."

Right now you are terrified of this thought of "going with the flow." You even have a saying, "Only dead fish go with the flow." You are missing the point here. Going with the flow is not simply letting life do with you what it will. Going with the flow is moving with the energy and not fighting it. You may be moved by energy and end up in a very good place. You may also be blocked by energy for a very good reason. Do not be so quick to judge flowing with life and not fighting against life. Often you are fighting and struggling and you simply exhaust yourself and wear yourself out.

How many of you are exhausted by your efforts to control everything? How many of you argue and fight with those you profess to love, in an effort to get them to do it your way? How many of you end up angry and frustrated simply because things aren't going your way? You can let go of all the struggle in your life by "allowing" yourself to "accept" and to "go with the flow." Sometimes the best thing you can do for yourself is to just stop pushing and pulling at your life. It would be a very good idea to simply calm down and breathe. Are there problems in the world? Yes! Do you have to fix them all? No....

You are simply a light being who was invited to this dimension and you are just passing through. You are simply a guest and I expect you to stay calm and act out of kindness, gratitude and respect!

As you evolve into your own godliness, you will leave behind some of your less desirable traits. You will begin to see the good in your journey here and you will begin to appreciate your fellow travelers.

You will come to a place of understanding that will surprise you and you will know things you have never before even thought about. As you evolve in this way, your awareness will gradually expand. You will have greater understanding and this great understanding will allow you to rise even higher.

As you rise, you continue to release the lower energies that have always been a part of you up until this point. These energies come to the forefront of your consciousness to be seen and then released. You do not send these thoughts and beliefs and ideas away from you, you simply *release your hold* on them. This allows these lower energies to move on and this allows you to "let go and flow." It is most difficult to move in an upward direction when you are holding on to an anchor.

So, as you "let go and flow," you will not only be releasing you from your anchor, you will literally be "letting go." The trick to letting go is to overcome your fears. If you can let go of fear, you can rise up in leaps and bounds.

So, what are your fears? How do you support your fears by holding them close to you and how do you nurture your fears? Do you go into your fears or do you keep anything and everything that you fear at a distance. Fear can be as small as "concern" and as large as "attack." You may have concern that your neighbor might steal your fruit from the tree in your yard, or you may attack your neighbor for stealing fruit from the tree in your yard.

You all carry fear and concern for your safety and you all carry concern and fear regarding finances. You may not worry directly about money, however, you do concern yourself with the availability of funds and how much your boss does or does not value you. If you are the boss, you more than likely have fears and concerns as to how much your customers value you or your product. In the same way that the economy runs countries, your personal finances run a good portion of your life. You are directly connected to violence and war and economic dishevel by your reliance on financial gain.

So, as we move forward we must learn that fear is a problem for us. Fear causes us to do things we normally would not do. Fear starts wars and fear energy is quite strong here on planet earth. Fear is a motivator in many situations and fear is even helpful in certain instances. Fear may push you to run to get out of the way when a typhoon or hurricane is coming. Fear can motivate and fear can stimulate your flight response.

As you continue to go within and learn to *trust* the God *in* you, you will be releasing your internalized fears and concerns. Your worry level may rise and this may simply be a response to the fear you are *letting go* of. Trust will assist you at these times. Trust God, trust yourself and trust the light being in you. Do not be afraid! Stay calm in all situations and "focus." Focus on the outcome itself, not on the fear or concern. Know that everything will be okay and know that everything is in divine order.

Tell yourself repeatedly to "just breathe" and *allow* yourself to go with the flow without getting all riled up or even all depressed. You are dealing with energy here. You, the light being, entered a body in this three-dimensional world to experience through the five senses. This is your great adventure! You wanted to come here. Let go and go with the flow. Nothing is really that serious. It's like you went to Disneyland and now you are afraid of the rides and the characters and all the people.

You on earth are becoming so afraid that you are shutting down and turning off your love. Your love is your greatest power and now you are losing your power. Turn your power back on! Turn you back on! Begin to love again! Begin to trust again! You came to earth for a reason. Go within and ask what you came here for and go in that direction. I am certain you have *chosen* to live on earth for a reason. You could have gone a billion other places. You chose earth. The light being *in* you chose this place. Let go of your fear of this place and begin to embrace it. This is a play and you are simply wearing a costume and acting out a role. Your character can become anything you choose. Let your role be great and perfect and wonderful. Enjoy this experience and stop complaining about it.

Life is made up of energy. You are energy. You create by interacting with energy. Create magic by allowing magic to be part of your awareness. Create wonder by allowing wonder to be part of your awareness. You get more of what you are in this three-dimensional world. The more love (and less fear) you are, the more love (and less fear) you create. The more joy you focus on, the more joy you get back. You all focus on things and money to bring you joy and love. Try focusing on joy to get more joy, and love to get more love.

This will allow you to move in a whole new direction. Joy brings joy into your life. Love brings love into your life. You are like a giant magnet and you attract what you are. You are what you focus on. Focus on the light being in you. Light is the highest vibration. Light brings more light, and light dissipates or dissolves fear. Know this and you will raise yourself up a notch and, in doing so, you will raise earth up a notch!

***

So, as you continue to evolve in awareness, you will continue to raise your vibration. Awareness is a form of enlightenment, and enlightenment is your goal.

As you become an enlightened being, you lose your need to fight and you lose your need to act-out. Most of you fight and argue out of the need to be right. You want to be the one in control so that you need not feel frightened. When you feel frightened or afraid, you are most uncomfortable. You lose your cool and you begin to harm others or you simply cause damage to inanimate objects. Anger is a direct result of frustration. Frustration comes from not having things go your way. In a way, anger is simply a temper tantrum. When you are quite large, your anger can be seen as very terrifying to others. If you have a weapon in your hands, you are then most terrifying.

So, how do we get you to calm down and become peaceful? We teach enlightening information that will lift you "up." When you are no longer fearful of life, you will become a more loving human. When you are afraid, you are pulling you down. Trust will help you to stay "up" in the higher vibrating streams of energy. Do not worry about those who are still in their anger and frustration and misunderstanding. Bring you "up," and in doing so, you will have an effect on them. This is due to the fact that you are energy. Energy communicates with energy and has a direct effect on energy. Every atom communicates with every other atom.

You, as a whole, are constantly communicating with the world that you live in. You, as an individual, are constantly communicating with the world that you live in. You literally affect the world around you and you affect those you are closest to. I would highly suggest that you begin to understand how you work in order to understand how energy works.

You are directly connected to everyone and

everything on this planet. You are running energy through you and this energy goes out and circles this planet and it affects the air that you breathe and it affects the trees and plants, and it affects the people and animals that are here visiting with you. You are literally *affecting* everyone and everything with the energy that you send out into this world that you live in. Please do not send more anger and frustration and fear. Please begin to send out love and kindness and understanding.

You say you cannot understand stupidity and rage and evil, and I will tell you that you are very lucky if you do not feel these emotions. This world has been subjected to years and years and years full of hostility and war. You fight and you argue and you disagree and you criticize, and all this dense energy is cracking some of you wide open. Others are sinking into despair and depression.

It is time to change! No matter what you see; no matter what you hear on your news, I want you to *choose* to feel love and compassion and kindness towards all involved. Do not get all riled up and start sending out more anger and rage, as these energies are circling this planet and they are pulling you "down." They cannot possibly lift you "up" simply because they are denser and slower vibrating energies.

You have the "power" within you to raise you "up." Once you raise you up a notch you begin to affect the air and the earth and the others who live here on earth. You! The single cell vibrating at a higher level will begin to communicate to the other cells within this giant body of humanity and will be sending a signal that is positive and uplifting.

This is how you raise humanity and this planet. It has taken many years of war and anger to get you this low, and it all began with fear. Please let go of your fear of life and your fear of danger and your fear of loss. I know this is most difficult for you, but if you could just move a little closer to trust, it would be most helpful. Let go of your fear of death, as you never ever die. You know this on some level and you know that you are simply a light being who came here to visit in this material world. You came for fun and games and to put on a show. You are light beings playing in matter. You have forgotten that you are this powerful creative being who creates. How do you create? You create by sending out energy from you!

As you learn how to connect with the higher-in-vibration parts of your own self, you will be configuring your own self in a whole new way. Transformation is a way of changing and transforming all parts of the whole body. Transformation includes the mind and spirit as well as the human form.

So, as you transform, you may *feel* this shift that is taking place *in* you. You may feel like you are uneasy or unsettled in some way and you may experience subtle, or even strong, body or emotional signals. When you disrupt the denser energies that have occupied you for so many years, those denser energies will be felt. Just know that these denser energies are being felt simply because you have dislodged them from their dormant stage and they are now able to move and to exit the body and/or mind. These dormant energies could erupt in emotional tension or even fear and upset. Most common are suppressed emotions and feelings which tend to rise to the surface at times of stress.

So, as you transform by lifting yourself up to experience the light in you, do not be too concerned if you release some long-held tension and stress. This involves staying calm and not going off half cocked insinuating that the worst is happening. The worst is not happening. In actuality, the best is happening. You are clearing and releasing the denser energies that show up as fear, anger, revenge, resentment, criticism and depression. These energies are in direct opposition to the higher vibration energies of love, joy, enthusiasm, peace and acceptance (also known as gratitude and appreciation).

As you release your hold on the lower vibrations they will, or may, rise up to be released. This allows you to clear them out of the way so they no longer *block* the higher vibrations. Lower energies are lower only because they vibrate much slower. Higher vibrations vibrate much faster. Lower vibrating energy can be thought of as an anchor that holds you down. Let go of your anchor and you rise up.

Now, as you know, you are a creative light being living inside of a body that is human and unaware of your presence. This light being is creative in nature. This light in you sends out signals and is always with you. This light being is *aware* that you (the human you) are unconscious and unaware on so many levels. This light being is God in you waiting for you to "wake up." This light being in you does not push and has infinite wisdom and patience. For God there is no time; there is no rush; there is no danger. Think of God waiting for you to wake up as yourself waiting for a big beautiful flower to bloom. You know that when this flower opens up it will be lovely and beautiful in color.

So, God in you waits patiently for you to wake up and to be all that you can be. God in you is guiding you by being with you and watching over you. When you begin to transform yourself by becoming *aware* that you are indeed a light being, you begin a *shift* within you that causes the *shift* in your energies within. This shift is felt by you and you release dense energy in whatever way is necessary. Not only are "you" waking up at this time, but many of you are waking up. Not everyone will feel what you feel, as your truth (better known as what you hold on to) is, or may be, different from their truth. This is due to the fact that you each have your own individual identity and are allowed "free will" within this dimension. Free will gives you the choice "without condemnation." Free will is a gift to each of you. God does not sit here and judge you for using your free will to make choices. God is not a pacifist and God is not vengeful. There is no wrath of God and there is no fiery place of punishment.

God is patience that is unlimited and expansive. God is eternal and does not know time.

So, as you continue to be part of God, I wish you to remember that you are timeless and you have no agenda other than to be exactly who you are. You are love and you are light. Everything else is an energy that can dissolve away in an instant. Yes! You are transforming and you are shifting in a whole new direction. Yes! This is being felt by some as strong change. Yes! You are affecting everyone around you, and yes, they are affecting you.

This is what you do. You are all connected and you do not realize that you are. You have such a vast body that you do not realize that, when you meet them, you are actually meeting you. You are meeting another part of you. You are all cells within the same body and you are attacking one another and this is causing problems for this planet that you inhabit. You are fighting out of fear! Please let go of your fear and calm down so that *you* might rise up to the higher vibrations of love and joy.

Remember, fear is an anchor, and to rise up you must let go of this anchor. You are a light being, you are not this body that you inhabit. This body is a reflection of all that is in the mind. The mind is in every cell of this human body and you (the light being you) are in every cell of this body.

Allow you (the light being you) to be in control for a while. Allow you (the light being you) to call the shots. What? Are you afraid that you will sit around all day acting all pleasant and peaceful and loving? Would that be so bad???

When you become aware of your own divinity, you will be most amazed. Most often you do care for yourself, yet you are often putting yourself down. When you put you down, you are putting you at a disadvantage. If you can stay "up," you will benefit a great deal.

You rise and you fall on a daily basis and this is part of the rhythm of life in this dimension. Life on earth is not so difficult once you get the hang of it. You seem to get into trouble whenever you have a downward movement in your energy field. If you can just see how life moves in waves, it will be easier for you to ride these waves.

In addition to moving in waves, your energy also spirals up or it spirals down. This is determined by the energy that you take "in" and how you process it or how you *decide* to see it. This is known as perspective. So, now we have you taking "in" energy and processing energy, and converting this energy into a "positive" (something you like) or a "negative" (something you do not like). This processing is constant and continual. You process day and night. You are like a little creating machine that never shuts down.

Once you become *aware* of your power to create, you will begin to "allow" more of life to be okay, and this will lead to an acceptance of life. Once you can accept it, you can change it. If you constantly reject it you are constantly pushing it away. If you accept it, you may then "receive" it and begin to work with it, to change it into something "lighter." Do you wish to lighten and brighten your life? I highly suggest you begin to see how absolutely everything is acceptable, which will lead to absolutely everything becoming lovable. Yes! I know… the thought of everything being okay and then moved up to lovable is absolutely horrifying to you now.

You will find that acceptance *is* unconditional love of all that *is*. Acceptance, throughout all of the information I have written for you through Liane, has always been defined as love. So, as we move forward, I would like to see you let go of some of the grievances you hold against life on earth. You come to this playground to take part in the adventure and the limitations presented here, and then you get all upset and hurt because life on earth is exactly that. I would like you to view life on earth as you would any adventure. You are here to visit. You are not here to judge and condemn. Judgment and condemnation pull you down by their density. Acceptance and joy lift you up by their lightness.

As you continue to accept "life on earth," you may begin to see it as a movie or play that you (the light being in you) have stepped into simply for the fun of it. When you step into a part in a movie you do not sit around all day and complain. You simply work on your part and how to perfect it. You do not tell the other actors how to play their roles and you do not judge how the others are acting out their roles. As a matter of fact, you haven't seen the entire script, you don't know the twists and turns in the plot, and you definitely do not know the roles the other actors may be playing in this movie.

For someone who is totally unaware and doesn't know what's going on here in this particular dimension, you certainly do complain a lot. So, we are now going to give you some guidance, which will hopefully allow you to accept life more and maybe even let go of some of your fear of life here on planet earth!

As you continue becoming all that you can be, I wish you to know that you are not ever punished. This nonsense about God punishing his children really needs to stop. There is no judgment day and there is no bad side to karma. Everything is simply energy and you are all simply energy also. Energy reacts with energy in specific and non-specific ways.

Once you *realize* how everything is actually given a name or meaning by those who are observing it, you will begin to see how *you* create your own personal reality by how you judge it or how you name it.

Say you get into a car accident. You may begin to wonder what you have done wrong in order to cause such a situation, or you may "look for the good" in this situation. The bad could be the expense of fixing your new, but now damaged, car. The bad could be the time you must now spend repairing your vehicle. So now you have created a bad situation that you *believe* you have somehow caused and you are depressed for days.

Flip to another perspective and look for the good in this situation. The good is that this accident was set in motion to occur because of the energy flow here in this dimension. The good and best thing is that you are un-injured and safe. The good thing is that no one died (although that would not be awful as we have been learning). The good thing is that there are people called mechanics who love fixing damaged vehicles. The good thing is that you may choose to see this whole incident as a good thing instead of a bad thing.

In making this choice to see this instance as "good" you allow yourself to ride a wave of "good" energy, which is much lighter than a wave of "bad" or denser energy. You are an energy being who is constantly moving with, and interacting with, the energy of this dimension. You get to decide whether you ride a wave up, or whether you ride it down by spiraling down. Everything presented here can be used as a "gift" to allow you to ascend or to descend.

Once you go down a bit, you may always choose to go back "up" by allowing yourself to see how this is a playground where *you* decide how it will look to you! See the good in absolutely everything and you will have a most enjoyable time here on earth. This is not a place of war and judgment and condemnation unless *you* decide to see it as such. You *chose* to come to a place that shows you what you choose to see. This planet is similar to Disneyland in that you may go to Fantasyland and ride in a teacup or you may go to Frontierland and see a real live shootout at the O.K. corral. Do not try to stop the bad guys from shooting everyone unless you wish to become part of that play. If you belong in Fantasyland in a spinning teacup do not involve yourself in what is going on over in the Pirates of the Caribbean.

It is all a play! You are involved in this three-dimensional world because you chose to come here to experience all that you are experiencing. It is as though you put on a blindfold to play Pin the Tail on the Donkey and now that you are blindfolded and have been spun around, you are afraid, simply because you do not know where you stand and where things (unseen things) are; and you want out of this game.

Here is your way out. Sit down, be very, very calm, and just breathe! Do not try to fix things. Do not criticize things! Do not get involved in things just for the sake of being involved. Sometimes you feel so unloved and so left out of acceptance that you try to fit in by getting "involved" with energy that has nothing to do with you. Stay uninvolved with the outer world and get involved with your inner world. Outside of you is just the projected image. Inside is the universe that is you.

You figure that out while I have a little chat with Liane….

※

You are always going to question and wonder. You are in a human body that allows you to think and to dream and wonder about your awareness. As you continue to question who you are and why you came here, you will be opening up to new ideas and new perspectives.

You are not here for no particular reason. You each have your reason for coming even if that reason is simply curiosity. So, if you have come here for a reason, don't you think that you should begin to calm down with your judgments and get a little more trusting regarding this *decision that you have made?* I would suggest that you become a little more observant and a little less critical. So, as you watch your daily news, I would caution you to not get too riled up about every little and even big thing. If you cannot watch the news or read the news without getting your emotions all worked up, I would highly suggest that you turn off your television and put down your reading.

It is not necessary to get you all fired up about war and disease, as it will only cause greater confusion and dense energy to circle this planet. When you take in information that riles you up, you get all upset and sometimes you even become afraid of the future by doing so. You are an energy being and you create! How do you create when you are afraid and confused and upset? You send out energy that is upsetting and confusing and fear-filled. I am trying to get you all calmed down here. I know you all want to be an activist and do good for the world. I would prefer that you stop all the rhetoric, and become a little more peaceful before you begin judging situations and spouting off about your good opinion. I am not asking you to lie down and let everyone walk all over you, I am asking you to sit down and shut up until you have something good and positive and wonderful to say. This will begin to send good, positive, wonderful energy out into the world.

The earth and animals and all of nature have been bombarded with negative energy for eons. Let's shift the energy up a notch and begin to send positive uplifting energy out of *you*. You may "lift" the energy surrounding you and your loved ones. All energy goes out from you and circles this earth and comes back to you. You are like a magnet, as energy always returns to its sender. You will be receiving your good vibrations as you continue to send more good vibrations out into the atmosphere.

Calm is good, and high, and light in its vibration. Happiness and joy are even higher. If you cannot stay in happiness and joy, try acceptance. Unconditional acceptance is equated here with unconditional love of life on earth. You may continue to judge and bring you down, or you may become the *observer* and look at the situation until you find something *good* in it.

You see a shooting on your news and you get all upset and sad and angry at others; not just the shooter but anyone related to him and anyone who befriended him. This upset and angry energy is strong judgment that is sent out and circles the earth and affects people and nature and even the earth. So, how do you respond in a better way? You may start by sitting down and keeping any negative thoughts to yourself if you are upset. If you have already learned the art of unconditional love and acceptance, your energy will not be so dense and you will not have the urge to go off half angry and totally upset.

So, you sit down and shut up and *observe.* Watch the situation and notice any good that comes from it. Does it bring people closer together? Do people want to help others? Do people become loving and kind towards complete strangers? Do people hunger for peace and love? You will find the good if you look long enough. History has a way of teaching this planet what is really helpful and what is not so helpful. Right now you are sending out energy that is not so helpful. Do you want to do your part? Stay calm and you will be assisting in a very big way.

---

*Y*ou will learn how to use your creative energy in a positive way and this will allow you to have peace in your life. This will also allow you to be happier and to know love. Love comes to you in many forms and you often choose not to see it. When you are loved, you are accepted. Often you do not wish to be accepted by certain individuals. You only wish to be accepted by those you value in some way. If they have no immediate value to you, you do not care whether they accept or love you. If you do not care, you usually do not feel their love and acceptance. This puts you in a position of feeling a shortage in your love life. You cannot seem to get enough love and acceptance, and this is due to *your* lack of giving love and acceptance.

Once you begin to give out love and acceptance, you will begin to *feel* loved and accepted. So, let's start with your own personal world. Do you love and "accept" your family or do you wish they would go away? Do you wish they were different than how they are, and do you wish they would change? This is the same as non-acceptance or wanting this current version of them to leave so you might have a different, more likable version.

So, if you reject them, you reject you! If you reject them, you will *feel* rejection in your life simply because *you* are a creative being who has chosen to send out the energy of rejection. Remember – there is no right way or wrong way to create! There is only energy. You are energy and you send out energy. No right or wrong. No good or bad unless *you* decide it is.

So, we have you not accepting and causing you to be sad and feel rejected, and left-out, and not-as-good-as the others who are visiting earth. Most of you can easily change this situation. You have so much confusion around love and what it is, or is not, that I will suggest you use acceptance as a way of changing this part of your life.

What do you reject? Do you reject trends and fads? Do you reject people whose skin color does not match yours? Do you reject those who are very wealthy? Do you reject those who are very poor and live in squalor? Who do you reject? What do you reject? You came here for diversity of creation. You, the light being in you, came here to experience this diverse world. There are other dimensions you may visit that do not have the diversity of earth. If you hated black people, would you choose to visit South Africa? If you hated the Chinese, would you choose to visit China? You came here knowing how diverse this earth world is. Why not accept it and embrace it as is? Why cause yourself problems by not accepting the terrain? You create problems for yourself by the energy that you run through your body on a daily basis.

Do you want to *feel* loved and accepted? Love and accept life "as is" as much as you can and whenever you can. You have become so stingy with your tolerance and your acceptance that it is creating problems for you. You accept people who sometimes abuse you, in an attempt to receive much wanted love and validation. You continue to reject those who have done nothing to you and to accept others who might abuse you in various ways. You live in a constant state of confusion.

I will make this very clear and simple for you. If he or she beats you – leave! Do not reject and mistrust everyone on earth because one or more have caused pain. Accept the majority as good and allow the one or more to be who they are meant to be, and move on. Unless you are an officer of the law and can officially make changes do not get involved.

Yes! I said do not get involved. You are all so confused and unaware of how you are causing your own problems, that your best course of action, if you are looking for love and acceptance in your life, is to not get involved in conflict. Leave if you are being abused physically or even emotionally. Do not look back and definitely do not seek revenge. Take care of you and do not cause you greater distress by wanting to see them get their just punishment. Revenge is a hard and heavy energy that will stick to you and color your own personal perspective of life. Revenge is causing problems for many of you, and it will pull you down out of the higher vibrating energies of love and acceptance.

Fear and rejection cause problems also. Let go of fear, as fear is the opposite of love. So this means you must let go of *fear of the future*, which is one of your favorites. So, love and accept if you want to *feel* love and acceptance. Reject and fear if you want to *feel* rejected and fear-filled. Revenge will simply pull you down and eventually suffocate you so that you are unable to *feel* the higher energies of love, peace and joy.

You get to choose, each and every moment of each and every day, how you will *experience* this dimension. If you wish to go "up" and *feel* joy, love, acceptance and peace, you may choose to do so. If you wish to stay where you are, you may do so. I support you in your choices. I *accept* you as you are. If you choose to go "down" energy wise, you may do so. You are simply traveling through the inner dimensions of a very vast creation. The universe is within you and you are simply exploring all that is.

You will find that your journey is the reason you came here. You came to earth for the experience and the challenges and the fun of creating in this way. You lose consciousness as you come in, but you knew that before you dove in. You are an explorer and you have chosen this place for its diversity. Enjoy it, accept it, have fun with it. Test yourself. See how high you can go, simply by projecting your energy "up." You are here to enjoy the sights, not to judge and condemn and reject all that you see.

There is no wrong in what you do… not ever. You are watched and loved and accepted, "just as you are," beyond your wildest dreams. Stay on earth or leave earth, it does not matter. You are simply a light being wearing a costume. Right now you are unaware of your power to create so I am giving you suggestions that may assist you. None of these suggestions is law! There is no law in God's reality. There is only love and acceptance, mixed with an unending patience and understanding. You simply lack understanding from where you are, so you have become fear-filled. Let it go… let all fear go….

*F*rom the time you first entered your body, you have been learning. You (the light spirit you) have been learning to operate this human form. You have been driving a car without any instructions. You have been operating without guidance.

You are here and you don't know why. You are in a human form and you don't know why. You are on earth and you don't know why. To say that you are unconscious is not much of a statement. You are totally unaware of who you are and no one has given you instructions on how to proceed. Because you are unaware, you have become disconnected from your source. It is time to return! You are about to move in a whole new direction and this new direction is toward open awareness.

Awareness frightens you, simply because you do not understand that knowledge is power. I am not speaking here of intellectual knowledge. I am speaking of intuitive wisdom. Some things you just *know* and it has nothing to do with how intelligent you may or may not be.

As you grow in awareness, you may become a little unsettled and uneasy. You are literally being dislodged from a position that you have been *stuck* in, and now you are moving in a whole new direction. For many of you this new direction will be "up." This is due to the rise in speed, or vibration that is now affecting earth's entire atmosphere. Things are changing as they are meant to. Earth is moving and you are moving. You are energy and earth is energy. Energy is all that really exists, and for now, this energy that is part of absolutely everything is on the rise. It is speeded up in an effort to assist you in this game that you play called life.

This game has been going on for eons and now it is time to shift up to the next level of awareness. Since time does not really exist, you are acting out your roles over and over in various dimensions and within a specific grid. You do not live one life as a caveman and then come back for your next life a few hundred years later. Time is not linear but is occurring instantaneously. You might be a businessman or woman in a high rise building in one life and come back your next life as a cave dweller who carries a club for a weapon.

Time is not linear and all time is occurring instantaneously! You may be in more than one lifetime at any given time. You may be experiencing these lifetimes simultaneously. How? You are all one giant body and you have focused your energy down so that you only see portions of *you* at any given time.

So, as your attention is focused on this you (who is reading this book) you will relate to this you and be upset by anything that may go wrong in the life of this you. What about the life of the other you's who may be out there? Do you care about them and their welfare? No – not so much! You are focused solely on you, as this is how the game of life on earth is set up. If you enter the bodies of more than one human at any given time, are you responsible for those other you's? And what if one or more of your other you's lives in a neighboring country that you despise? Or what if one of your other you's is right next door and you hate them for whatever reason? Be careful how you treat others, as your thoughts not only affect your cells in your body, they also affect the earth and everyone on it. They are energy that is sent out into the atmosphere and they eventually return to their sender.

Then we have your actions? Do you bully your neighbors or people you know? What if they are one of your you's? Do you hate certain individuals for their beliefs or politics? What if they are *you*?

So, you can see how interconnected everything is when it comes to energy. Where do you begin and where does your neighbor end or begin? Where are the boundaries when it comes to energy? Is a light being totally enclosed within the human body, or does it extend beyond the body? Are you an energy being within a body or are you an energy field surrounding and within the body? And how many bodies can you inhabit at one time? The answer to that is "many." You may operate more than one human form at any given moment. And since time does not really exist, you may be doing this simultaneously.

So, back to my original discussion regarding *you* moving in a whole new direction. As you shift directions, you become more and more aware of your connection to absolutely everything. You are being moved to awareness by the amount of light that is entering this dimension. The more light that enters, the easier the shift upward becomes. In the beginning, as you begin to become aware of your oneness, you will feel pulled and a little uncomfortable. You have been stuck in the lower energies for some time now and you might say that you have become attached to vibrating a little slower. You have grown some roots here if you know what I mean? You have settled into this slow unconscious energy and as you begin to open up and become more aware, you will be pulling your energy up and out of the solidity that it has attached to. No more being stuck and stubborn. We are moving up to the free-flowing energy of flexibility.

You cannot hold judgment when you are free-flowing and flexible in your perception of life on earth. You cannot stay stuck once you become fluid, you cannot stay down once your roots have melted away. Let go of all that you currently hold on to and you will begin to rise up. "Live and let live! Go with the flow of the energy of your life," and do not hold on to the old way of judgment and fear.

You are moving up! You are reconnecting with

your source which contains only love and acceptance for all!

※

*Y*ou are only one of many species who come here to experience life on earth. You are all connected and yet you *feel* separate from all that come. You are not separate. You are each an individual expression of the same source. You each flow back to the same source.

If you were to look at how your lives have been formed, you would believe that you are completely different in nature. However, when you trace each of you back through time to the original incarnation, you all came in as a group consciousness with the desire to express yourselves in this dimension. You may look individual but you are all connected at your source. In the same way that your mind can express many thoughts in a day, your source may express in many, many ways.

So, as you continue to learn and grow in awareness, it is most important to remember that you are all connected and you are basically all cells within the living body of God. To heal the body, one must attain a healthy balance. This is my intention! This is why I rouse Liane from her sleep to write for me. We are working here to bring you into balance and to promote the healing of *you*. You – this individual cell within the body of God is in deep distress and is asking to receive guidance. You – this individual cell is in trouble and requires assistance. You would not be reading this material if you were not meant to read it. This material is meant to guide you back into balance and you have been guided to it for a reason.

I am not asking the entire earth population to stop everything and sit down and shut up and breathe. I am asking *you* to sit down and shut up and breathe. The rest of the world is being guided from within to do what is necessary for their current role that they are playing here on earth. The rest of the world is just fine acting-out and playing and entertaining themselves in this illusory world.

You are the one who is requesting guidance. *You* are the one who has been guided to read this information. I don't care if someone else gave you this book or if you are only reading it because it was a gift! You are the one being guided to read this material. If your true intent is to heal and to balance, you may not even know this on a conscious level. You may require balance and healing, and your guidance is just so strong that it has guided you to this information.

So, do not be concerned that if everyone sits down and shuts up, and simply breathes and enjoys life that nothing will be accomplished. Oh! Wait! Maybe that *is* what *everyone* needs to do! This entire planet in meditation... wouldn't that be a lovely sight....

As you continue to become aware of your true nature, you will be opening up to the origins of earth. You will begin to see how you originally created this playground and how some have forgotten that it is indeed a playground. You began to create rules to stifle your creativeness and now it is time to let go of some of your rules.

You need not be so hard on yourself and you need not be so controlling. Your controlling nature is a direct result of the amount of fear that you carry. You are fearful simply because you are afraid. You are afraid of life and you are afraid of death. I have an assignment for you today. I would like you to make a list of at least 20 things that you fear. Your list may include insects, wild animals, storms, types of death such as drowning, disasters, diseases, any little or big thing that you fear. Do not forget to list phobias and emotional fears such as abandonment. Do you fear angry people? Do you fear the homeless and the drug addicted? Do you fear hospitals? Do you fear courtrooms and police stations? Do you fear traffic cops and gang riots?

Your list may be as long as you like. I want you to get in touch with your fears in order to know how full of fear you are. Then we have the biggies, like fear of not being in control. Fear of not being loved and accepted. List your fears and begin to *know* who you are and what energy you might carry. Next I want you to go down your list and try to *accept* one of your fears. You may accept a fear by looking at it and seeing it differently then releasing it. You might look at your fear of not being wealthy. How can you see this fear differently? You might begin to see the ways that not having wealth have added to your life. I am not asking you to not strive for abundance here. I am asking you to let go of your fear regarding poverty and maybe even homelessness.

So, if you look at how not having wealth has added to your life, you may find the "gift" in being exactly where you are financially. Say you live in a nice enough home but you do not have the finances to afford a cleaning service or yard service. You must do all cleaning and yardwork yourself. A side benefit of doing housework and yardwork is that you stay in good physical condition. Some of you who work day-in and day-out in an office would *prefer* to have some physical movement during your day. Another benefit is breathing. When you breathe from exertion, you literally take in more oxygen which feeds the blood and exercises the heart.

I know – if you were a millionaire, you shout! You would simply join a gym. Maybe, but would you follow through and go? Anyway, we are looking for the "gifts" in the life that you now have. We are looking at our fears in order to own our fears so we might release our fears.

If you fear hurricanes you might focus on how neighbors come together and assist one another after total devastation. You might focus on how many are helped by the Red Cross and other government agencies. Life does eventually return to normal and you do go on. And please remember when facing your fears regarding death, that you go on and on and on and on for eternity!

So, now I have made you uncomfortable with this information regarding your fears. When fear comes to the surface, you hate it. When fear comes to the surface, you try to push it back down. I would like to see you allow it to surface in order to allow yourself to release it. If you can just release a little fear you will be a little lighter. Fear is quite dense and fear energy is like a weight in you. The more you can allow fear to come to the surface, the greater your chance of releasing your hold on fear. You cannot release your fears if you do not acknowledge them and then allow them to be.

You do not release fear by hiding it deep *in* you. You may list your fears and this will tell you how fear-filled you are. Then you might look at how to find something positive about each fear. Trust me on this, there will be a "gift" in each situation. If the fear is a biggie like death, the gift is the fact that you move on and continue as a light being.

So, now I would like to assure you that you are not creating greater fear by acknowledging what is *in* you. As a matter of fact, it will be like releasing a long-held secret shame. When you bring these denser energies to the surface with the "intent" of healing, you are beginning a process of healing. Remember, you are a creative being and you create what you focus on. Focus on healing and being healed. Focus on releasing fear and letting it go.

You do not heal and balance by holding on to the dense energy that pulls you down. You heal and balance by letting go and rising up. Let the fear go and allow its opposite, which is love energy, to enter you. Love is light and high. Fear is dense and low.

Now, once you have looked at your list of fears and found a "gift" in each one, I would ask you to thank your fearful thoughts for any service they have given you and then ask them to move on and go forward from you. This will allow your fears to leave you and you will be working with your fears instead of suppressing them and hiding them and pushing them deeper into *you*.

When you push your fears deeper into *you*, you literally stuff them into all your cells and atoms and anywhere within the body that you might hide them. This causes the cells and atoms *in you* to vibrate slower and this slows your entire vibrating system more. "Stress kills" has become a slogan of this modern age. Stress is a direct result of fear. Fear drives you to achieve more and do more – fear of what the neighbors will think, or fear of what the family will think. Let go of stress by releasing your fear. Begin to slow down and breathe. Just stop, please! I would like to see you return to love and operate from love. Love cannot exist when fear is present. Love is like a light and fear is like the dark. If you turn on your love light, you dispel the darkness.

Now, when you *decide* that fear is going to become your friend so that you might communicate with it and *allow* it to leave you, you will feel it as it surfaces. Allow your fearful feelings and do not judge them. Allow yourself to see "all" of you and to know "all" of you.

This will do for now as my pen (Liane) is having pain from being frozen in position to write this to you. She will feel better when she no longer writes regarding fear and death. These are two very big energies on earth and the body reacts to them in big ways.

For now, I will ask you to make your lists and allow yourself to release some of your fear energy; you will be so happy and much lighter after doing so.

The extent to which you will go to avoid fear is great! None of you enjoy feeling fear. Some enjoy the exhilaration of being a daredevil and doing risky stunts, however, this has become more of a game and less about facing your fears.

When you face your fears, you own them. Once you own them, you may change them into something less fearful. Say you have a fear of being shamed in public. Once you have experienced being shamed, you may become more adamant about this fear or you may *realize* that everyone makes mistakes and everyone is simply doing their best here on earth. If you decide to accept this fear and allow it to be less traumatic, you will literally be defusing its power over you. If you want to continue to be afraid of public shame, you may allow it to become a big drama that takes over your thoughts and, in doing so, takes over your energy field.

So, you are constantly deciding which direction you will travel by the choices you make. Positive, light, uplifting choices go "up." Negative, judgmental choices go "down." Again – you're energy. Thoughts are energy. You exist in an energy field. No right or wrong here! You are an energy being having an effect on "all" energy surrounding you and "within" you. You are a creative force that is meant to create. No one told you that you contain this element of creation, so how could you possibly know? You were told how you are human and how you are good if you do A, B or C and bad if you do X, Y or Z. You are not either. You are a light being who has entered a human form in order to *experience* matter.

As a light being you are unable to interact with matter. As a human being, you may freely interact with matter and nature. So you might enjoy the fragrance of a beautiful flower. You might enjoy the *feeling* of the breeze blowing through your hair. You might enjoy the sights and sounds of earth.

You have begun to lose your sense of enjoyment and I want to return you to it. So, to experience joy, you must release your hold on sorrow. What makes you sad? Does your list of fears from yesterday's assignment make you sad? Does your judgment against politics make you sad? Does your judgment against radical beliefs make you sad? Let them go! You are causing your own sadness by how you "see" this world that you live in. Not only do you cause your own sadness, you actually spread greater sadness by projecting this energy out into the atmosphere.

Begin to *realize* how you create and what you do. You are not here to pass judgment and you are not here to bring this dimension down. You are here visiting and you are here to create greater joy and to bring in a little more awareness. Those of you who are playing the role of the bad guy in this movie will learn to change your role when the rest of you no longer request an antagonist in your movie. You ask for and you receive. You ask for a villain by judging the energy as villainous. If you were to switch off your judgment, you would see much less violence. Violent thoughts and beliefs require violent energy to come forth. Hold your judgment please! The very things that you judge are *growing* with all the energy (power) that you are putting into them. You must begin to see how you create it all. Your violent, pushy, aggressive thoughts regarding your neighbors' behavior are giving more power to violence, anger and aggression.

It's cause and effect, people! Not cause and "you will get yours for doing this," but cause as in "energy out of you creates and comes back to you."

You will find that the best way to get yourself in a better position to create joy in your life is to sit down, shut up and breathe. Nothing else is required here. If you would all just sit down, shut up and breathe, you would be sending out calm, peaceful energy; and what kind of world would calm peaceful energy create? Yes, it would draw you into a calm and peaceful world.

You think on this while I speak with Liane about our day together….

※

*Y*ou will find that you most want to be judgmental when it comes to situations that cause you fear. Most often you are looking for something wrong. You are so afraid and mistrustful that you are constantly on the alert for anything that might go wrong.

I wish you to turn this energy around and go in the opposite direction. I want you to begin to focus on all the big and little things that go right for you each and every day. Like, you just read this and you are still breathing; you are breathing in and out and isn't that wonderful? And look! You just walked across the room on these glorious legs of yours. And wow! You can actually "see" through your own eyes to read this. You can move to another room and begin to clean or simply admire how it looks, simply because everything today has gone right. Your eyes opened this morning. You were breathing this morning. You may have made yourself breakfast this morning. You may have gone to the garage and driven your car to the store or to work.

All of these things went right. They were all good! They all helped you and supported you in your existence here today. Notice "all" the things that go right for you each and every moment. Stop looking for things to go wrong. When you "look for" things to go wrong, you will eventually "find" what you are looking for. You are becoming paranoid in your *search* for everything to fall apart. Stop judging your future and you will stop the "pull" of a dense and dangerous future to you. You draw to you that which you project out of you. If you project a positive happy thought, it's going to draw something positive and happy to you. It's all energy, people! It has nothing to do with good or bad/right or wrong. It is energy being sent out by an energy field that is "contained" within a human form. It is energy that goes forward into a vast energy field that contains absolutely anything and everything that could possibly be created.

You are sending your order, your desire, your magnetic belief out into the field of all possibilities and it will always return to its sender in some form. Be aware that you are energy. Be aware that you (the atoms and photons in you) communicate with all of creation. Everything is made of energy and energy communicates with energy. You are simply "unaware" of all that you are and all that you do.

For the Love of Life on Earth

❧

*Y*ou will find that life on earth is not all that difficult once you begin to embrace it. Most of you begin to shut off your romance with life once you grow out of childhood. You begin to lose your enthusiasm and you begin to judge life based on what you are taught and how you are *trained* to be an adult. Think about it! When you are a small child, you are content to climb a tree and play in the grass. You are content and happy to play in the dirt and to watch clouds float by. As you mature, you are trained to be proper young adults. You are taught how big boys and girls *should* behave. You are *trained* to be more sophisticated in your thinking and to be a little more discerning in your ideas about life. You have begun your descent into judgment.

Life is not set up to harm you and you are not trained by those who would see you be harmed. You are simply being trained by those who want to *protect* you from the dangers of life.

So now we have you in your teens and you are learning that to climb trees and play in the dirt and roll around in the grass is for children. All of a sudden being a child is now being judged. So you try your best to be more like the sophisticated adults and you follow their lead. You may even take on the role of an adult earlier in life. Most of you have had responsibilities laid on you fairly early in life and these responsibilities caused you to let go of childhood quite early. Sometimes you were in charge of younger siblings and sometimes your parents were simply not available to you.

So, you may have let go of your trust in life and your love affair with life quite early on. As you continue to learn to "accept" all that is and to sit down, shut up and breathe, I would like you to look around you. Look at the trees as their leaves blow in the wind. Go out into your yard and climb a tree; go out and roll around in the grass. Stick your face in a big beautiful flower. Be a kid again and play with nature. Be a part of life on earth in a more natural way. Be a child again and see the good all around you.

You need not stop being an adult, however; it would be a good idea to not be such a curmudgeon. Let go of being the top dog – the one in control – the one on top of everything. Become one with your inner spirit and begin to enjoy life on earth. You spend all your time working so that you might take a vacation to get away from your life. I would like to see you begin to "enjoy" your life by seeing the beauty and the magic that is all around you as well as "in" you. Turn off your news. Turn off your TV. Turn off your electronic devices and look up!

You are living in a magical, wonder-filled dimension and you are not seeing it for its beauty and its gifts. You only see it for what it can give you, and you take what you need and are not very grateful for all that this life in this dimension has given you. Appreciate life and let go of your judgment of life. You have fallen into a pattern of judgment that is quite harsh and quite deep. Come up out of judgment and "allow" everyone and everything to be "okay." You are the one who decides whether life is good or bad by how you judge life. Allow life to be okay "as is" until you can pull yourself "up" enough to stop all judgment from pulling you down.

⁂

So, as you continue to discover your own beingness, you will continue to wake up to the awareness that you truly are.

You are so much greater than you realize. Your light body is vast indeed. You go from here to there and you do not realize how you operate and how you travel out of body, and how you are interacting with others in other dimensions. You are this vast energy field, and you siphon off parts of your energy into different shapes and sizes and you call these "bodies" and "nature" and "worlds" and "dimensions." You leave energy and you continue to flow through "all" energy. You are part of this giant, vast, never-ending field of energy that contains "all" possibilities.

So, if you are this energy field, how is it that you feel so disconnected and fearful? You are in a state of amnesia. Say you were the king of the most powerful country and all of a sudden you became unconscious and you did not recognize your fellow royal court and you did not recognize your castle, and you were confused and unaware of how life on earth works.

All of a sudden this once royal head of state is now in a most disturbing position. He does not know his own power. He does not "realize" that what he says becomes law. He does not know who he is and therefore does not trust his surroundings. This is "you." You only know that you are in a strange land with people and rules you do not understand. You have lost your awareness, however, you still retain your ability to rule or "create."

Now that you are waking up, you will be less fearful and you will remember your power and you will be comfortable in the "awareness" of the role that you play in this life on earth.

So, do not be afraid that you will never wake up and come out of your unconscious state. You have begun this process and you will continue to grow in awareness and to be less and less fearful. Fear is a byproduct of unconsciousness. Fear is a byproduct of not knowing how you create and how you contain life "within" you.

You are so focused on your outer world, when all the action is taking place "within." You are creating your life and your world, and projecting it out onto the screen of your life. You are not the result so much as you are the cause. You may change what you see, or view, on the screen by changing the focus of energy that is coming from within "you." Let your focus be on what you love not on what you hate! Let your attention be on what you want not on what you don't want! You are the projector of this show, this movie that you are viewing. Change the movie by changing what you are projecting.

Now, for those of you who like to "focus" on your outer world, I would suggest you go to the source which is "within" you. You do not create from the outside in, you create from inside out. So, if you see it "in" your world, you are projecting it!

Say you see someone attack another. You get all upset and you becry how awful the world is and how awful this person is. In actuality, what you saw was a man having a seizure and flailing his arms about and striking another person in his seizing state. You, however, have projected out judgment and only see evil and violence and attack. It is similar to when a person is drowning and flailing in deep water. He may pull others down with him, however, it is not evil nor is it awful. *It is what happens when someone is in fear.*

So, stop projecting your personal judgments onto the viewing screen of your life. Be a little more compassionate and a little more understanding. You will find that if you begin to project out compassion and understanding, you will begin to see greater compassion and understanding in your own personal life.

You are the projector. You determine what you will see by how you "perceive" any given situation. Please start to project love – unconditional love – out onto the viewing screen of your life. I know it is difficult for the unconscious "human you" to understand this, but it is second nature for the "light being" you who resides "within" you and knows that absolutely everything is in divine perfect order.

You may choose. You may continue to view death as awful and terrible or you may come over to the light side and see how everything is perfect. You get to decide whether you will continue to judge and bring in more dense, slower energy or accept and allow the energy that you bring into this world to be a light, higher-in-vibration energy. You may continue to keep yourself down or you may "decide" to lift yourself up....

❧

*Y*ou will begin to discover your own good as you *allow* for good to be a possibility. Many of you carry low self-esteem and this is due to the judgments that you carry. When you judge the world as a bad place, you are running energy through *you* that says, "You are bad." When you judge yourself as bad, you are running energy through *you* that says, "You are bad." When you judge your neighbor as bad, you are running energy through *you* (your body) that says, "You are bad."

How do you expect to be in good emotional health with all this energy that is dense pulling you down? When you see life as good, you are running energy through *you* that says, "You are good." When you see your neighbor as good, you are running energy through *you* that says, "You are good." And when you see you as good, you will be running energy through you that says, "You are good."

Would you like to raise your self-esteem? This should be a good way to start.

Now, when you wish to change, you do not push at others to change. This is important. Pushy, aggressive energy creates problems for you. When you "push" at others you literally push at them or push them forward or away from you. Let everyone be and you will be allowing you to simply "be." This is how you get into trouble. You find something that works for you and then you begin to push "your way" onto everyone else. Do not push. Allow everyone to "see" what calm and peace look like by being an example of calm and peace. If this sounds a little simplistic, it is because you have forgotten how to simply "be" a light being. The light being in you knows calm and peace well. The light being in you knows patience without end. The light being in you *is* calm and peaceful simply because the light being *in* you sees the bigger picture.

  The light being in you knows it never dies. The light being in you knows it is exploring various dimensions simultaneously. The light being in you knows this earth life is all a projection of the process of perception. The light being in you knows it is always in existence and always will be. The light being in you sees how your life here on earth is a play; a movie that you are directing and starring in. The light being in you is unafraid and is aware. When you are unafraid and aware you do not require reassurance, you simply are aware of all possibilities. The light being in you is the best part of you. You may begin to merge with the light being in you by matching your energy with this part of you. How do you match your energy with this part of you? Become calm and be at peace. Do not be *afraid* to be calm and peaceful.

You on earth have been agitated and upset long enough. Please calm down and stop throwing your energy in all directions. You are an energy being! You are constantly projecting *your* energy out into the world for all to experience. Please calm down with your assessment of life on earth until you have greater *awareness* on this entire situation.

Peace and calm is all it takes. Breathe in peace… breathe out calm. This is your lesson for today. No matter what occurs during your day I want you to focus on just two energies… breathe in peace… breathe out calm….

❦

This entire experience (or trip to earth) has been a *choice*. You do not come here out of some big punishment or banishment. You come here for the fun of it and for the experience. You *know* you may encounter various conditions by choosing this level or dimension to explore. If you *chose* to experience "Frontierland" would you complain that everything is rustic and old? If you *chose* to experience "Fantasyland," would you complain that everything is fairy like?

You are where you *chose* to be. You came for fun, and if you are not having fun you are not *enjoying* your choice. This is yet another judgment against the light being that you are. I would like to see you begin to enjoy this adventure. You may enjoy this adventure by allowing yourself the "gift" of acceptance! Acceptance is actually unconditional love. Acceptance is a very big gift that you can give to yourself and to the light being *in* you.

You may find this trivial and even unacceptable information, however, when it comes to energy, things matter. As a matter of fact, simple things become matter. Simple little thoughts when projected out over the years create your material world for you. Simplicity matters and simplicity will help you now. Stay calm, and calm energy will become your norm. Stay uplifted, and before you know it your thoughts will change from "worry" to "everything will work out just fine." No matter what occurs in your day to day living, you may always stop and change the *direction* the energy coming from within you is flowing. Push things away and you push people and life away. Accept and embrace and you will be accepted and embraced.

Once you begin to see how your energy *allows* you to create, you will begin to look at yourself in a whole new way. Always appreciate yourself and you will be sending out appreciative energy. Always like yourself and you will be sending out energy that draws likability to you. If you continue to judge others, you may expect to be judged. "You only judge the idiots and the bad guys that you see on your television," you shout! Judgment is energy being run through *you*, and this judgmental energy will affect the cells in your body and then it will go out into your immediate surroundings and will affect your personal world by filling it with judgment.

Do "not," I repeat, do "not" jump on the judgment wagon simply because all your friends and neighbors and relatives are on it. Be yourself! Do not spout off about how you are changing and going in a new direction, as this may cause problems for you. Your friends and family may *feel* that you are leaving their group consciousness and this can cause stress for them. Simply make your changes "within" you, adjust your acceptance gauge, and continue your spiritual journey quietly. There is no need to boast nor to try to take everyone on this journey with you.

Once you have *decided* to change the direction your energy is going, you will begin to feel helped and guided in your daily life. You will no longer feel so alone and unloved and unappreciated. You will begin to feel like you have a choice in life and you are not simply struggling to survive this life on earth. Some of you struggle financially while others struggle emotionally to fit in and be accepted.

Once you learn how to *use* your creative energy, you will be more accepting of your own personal role on earth this lifetime. You knew before you came here that this playground is full of castles and royalty as well as hovels and poverty. You are told and taught, and programmed to believe that living in a castle is best and living in poverty is the worst experience. Here in this dimension, the energy is very strongly in place that suggests that your worth, your value as a human, depends on how wealthy you are and how much you own. If you have adopted this belief as your own, you may well have caused some undue stress on yourself this lifetime.

You hear often how wealthy people have the best in life, and yet wealthy people suffer from judgment quite often. Wealth is not a protective barrier and wealth has its own set of complications. You may choose wealth or poverty or anything in between. You will not be judged except by your own self. When you live in poverty, you do so out of choice. This could have been a choice that was made long before you entered this lifetime. This could also be a choice that was made after you entered this lifetime. Either way, your condition is acceptable and does not deserve judgment.

Now, when it comes to wealth you may make choices that will assist you in achieving wealth. I would be remiss here if I did not tell you that I have channeled information through Liane on this very topic. The book I wrote through her is titled, *For the Love of Money: Creating Your Personal Reality*. I highly suggest you read it for greater insight into the possibility of giving yourself the gifts of this world.

Now, when you judge yourself as not as good, or as valuable, as your neighbors, you become what I will call worthless in your own mind. When you have these unconscious thoughts that you are worthless, you *create* an environment where you do not deserve as much as others. You are literally making yourself worth "less" than others and so you give yourself less than others might receive. This worth "less" state can be changed by letting go of the judgments against yourself that have caused you to be put down energy wise.

So, how do we remedy this situation? We stop sending out judgment! So no more good guys and bad guys. No more this is better/this is worse. No more right/wrong. No more good/bad. Everything is simply energy and energy moves and energy creates and energy simply "is." Not good – not bad – just "is."

So, here is a little trick to use when you have the urge to judge. Simply say to yourself, "Well, it is what it is," until you see where the energy is going to take you. Once you see where the energy takes you, you may choose another attitude such as, "What will be, will be," or, "Everything will work out just fine, I trust God/life/spirit." Once you get yourself into a more trusting mindset, it will be easier for you to "go with the flow" of your life as your spirit planned it.

So, sit down, shut up and breathe in and breathe out. Once you have done this I want you to think positive thoughts like, "This will be okay in the end," or, "Everything will work out just fine." It's time to come out of worry and fear, and move into love and acceptance!

As you can see, it is most difficult to get you to a place of trust. You have existed in a state of mistrust for many years now. Most of you began to feel mistrustful around the time you became an adult. Some children are put in very challenging circumstances and become very fearful and mistrustful early in life. For the majority, however, mistrust is formed in early adulthood.

Think about your children and how free they are about expressing themselves. This freedom of expression is often squelched as parents and adults begin to train a child to "behave properly." What happens next is a whole set of energy shifts and changes as this child tries to become what society wants him or her to become. You then send your child to a school to learn the ways of human behavior. The ways of human behavior are basically "rules to follow to keep you safe." These "rules to follow to keep you safe" are embedded in you and are followed by most of you.

So, if you are trained and supported in these beliefs, don't you think it may cause some conflict within your belief patterns when I come along and say, "Everything is in perfect, divine order?" As you learn to "accept" and "allow" life to be good and well "as is," you will be allowing *you* to be good and well "as is."

Here is a little trick you can use when you think you are slipping back into fear and mistrust. You can stop yourself by saying, "Stop!" "Wait!" "Sit down and be calm." Just stop what you are thinking and change the thought from a fearful one to a "Let's wait and see what the end result might be before I judge this situation." Maybe – just maybe, you will begin to move yourself into a much calmer state of mind. One calm human being will project out calmness. One fearful agitated human being will project out fear and agitation. Fear and agitation lead to anger and conflict. Calm and peace lead to joy and love.

You literally get to choose each and every day whether you live in fear or love. The choice is yours. You don't have to follow the crowd. You are no longer being trained to be worried about life and the world. You are reading this material because some part of *you* is desperate for love, peace and joy. Don't let this opportunity to change your inner programming go by. Use this opportunity to grow and to move in an "upward" direction. I realize that the downward pull by a programmed society is great, however, I also see how great and powerful and godlike you currently are.

Do not be afraid to be you! Do not be afraid to be God. Do not be afraid to trust God and to trust life and to be free of fear. You can do this! You are a creative being and you have the ability and the capability to create love in place of fear. Love feels much better than fear, and love will nurture you and sustain you in ways that fear energy cannot!

---

*Y*ou are probably most interested in where you go and what you do after you leave your body in this particular life. I will tell you that it is totally different for every one of you. Many leave this dimension and go visit other selves existing in other dimensions. You often leave and stay partially connected to this earth plane until you *feel* comfortable moving on.

When you move on, you do so at your own

individual speed and with full support of the whole spirit/soul that is you. You might say that you always leave a great deal of your consciousness outside of your adventure into various dimensions. There is always the "observer you" watching over you. You are always connected to this greater part of you, and you are always communicating with this part of you through your thoughts and ideas and perceptions. You are never ever alone here on earth even when you *believe* that you are.

When you die, the only part of you that ends is your body. In actuality, your body doesn't really end either. Your body turns to dust or to ash and it nourishes the earth and nature. Plants and trees and flowers grow and feed animals and humans. You literally "become" a part of everyone and everything. You are all the same energy field to begin with, so this is simply a continuation of that "oneness."

As you continue to grow and nurture everyone as part of earth energy, you will become more and more "aware" of your connection to everyone and everything. You are growing *in* awareness now, as this is the time for you to become a little more conscious of who and what you are.

So, you do not end ever! Even your body will go on and "change" into something else. Change is all there really is because everything, absolutely everything, is energy. The rest of you, this living energy that is you, simply moves on! You do not really go anywhere because you do not travel outside of this energy field that you are part of. You stay "in" this energy field simply because there is nothing but this energy and it takes up "all time" and "all space." You are part of this field and you have the ability to focus down to the tiniest particle and "become" a living, breathing thought idea. You, the giant creative force, have the ability to shift the energy to a tiny pinpoint of light and create a form to encase this pinpoint of light, and then to enter this form and call it your creation.

You literally create matter so that you might enter matter! You then leave matter by letting your focus return to the grandness of your eternal existence as the expression of "all that is." You are everything and everyone! You are creating a focal point in order to express, in a tiny space, part of what you are. You are playing a game with yourself and this game has to do with going unconscious to your own vast greatness. You cannot play in this three-dimensional world without going down in your vast awareness and consciousness. It takes focus to get this tiny. To see, or create, such a small speck of light takes effort. Focus must be just right; then you are "in." "In what?" – you ask. In this three-dimensional game – in this world of illusion that is only a "dream;" a tiny pinpoint of light that you created and then entered. How did you enter? You put your "focus" on it. It is similar to when you daydream or have an "idea." One thought leads to the next thought and then to the next thought and so on and so forth, until you are "deep" *in* thought and you become unaware of your surroundings.

I am telling you now that you are deep "in" thought and you have created a "thought pattern" that is frightening you and making you angry. Back out of this thought pattern and raise your level of thought from fear energy to love energy. You are God creating as you go. You may make a completely new choice and begin to see life and death in a whole new way. No one dies and no one really exists….

As you learn to relate to life on earth as a soul instead of as a human with a fearful ego, you will begin to see life in a whole new way. You will begin to appreciate why you have come here and you will begin to see the beauty in each and every moment.

You often do not "accept" that you are wondrous and beautiful. But think about it! You are here in a body and you are totally unaware of your own divine presence "in" you. You are here to assist in this life and yet you feel like you are alone in all that you do. You are not alone! Your best friend, the best part of you, is right inside of you and you are totally unaware of this part. So, how do I wake you up to the wonder of you? This is why I contacted Liane. I decided to enter into a dialogue with the human ego in an effort to assist in this unconscious situation on earth. God *is* capable of communicating with the children of earth and they *are capable* of communicating with God.

This is how you will learn and grow in your future. Once fear has fallen away, you will not be so afraid to hear the voice of God. You will not be so afraid of situations that are beyond the five senses of your physical body. You are so much more and you are so much grander than you can possibly know at this point in time. As fear falls away, you will no longer be so afraid of the unknown. This will allow you to look for the good in all situations. Right now you are creating stress for yourselves over the simplest things and ideas. Let it all go and stay calm in all situations.

The world is not "going to hell in a hand basket." The world is just fine and dandy! The world is not out of tune so much as it is tilted and out of balance. It is leaning to one side and that is causing everything to "shift" to one side. It is leaning towards fear and away from love.

You may assist in bringing the world back into balance. "How" – you shout! I will tell you now, "lean towards love" in all your interactions during every moment of every day. Just that simple – "lean towards love" and you will tilt away from fear. You will send out energy into the atmosphere that will affect the earth's energy. Why will you affect the earth's energy? Simply because you are a creative energy being! You send out energy day in and day out. You have the ability to affect change simply by calming down and letting all criticism and judgment go. Can you do it? Will you do it? Do *you* care enough to do it?

❧

*F*or the most part you are disconnected from your source. You became so good at going unconscious in order to enter matter that you have now completely forgotten who you are. You are royalty and you sit in your fear and your mistrust and your criticism of self and others, and you are beginning to suffocate from carrying these energies.

I truly want to help you gain *insight* into how *you* are affecting not only the human body that you live in, but also your life on earth. You are inadvertently dragging you down with every little bit of criticism and judgment. If your goal in this life is to be happy, I highly suggest that you *stop your criticism!* You may stop by shutting off the part of your mind that is afraid and judging. You may shut off this part by catching it in the act. Each time that you think a criticizing thought, go back to that thought and find something good about the situation you are judging.

Sometimes you simply do not *understand* how souls come to earth to show you who you are. Sometimes large groups of souls come in, all at once, in order to teach the earth souls how to *accept* "all that is." Sometimes souls like to demonstrate how there really is no death, and so they will create a situation whereby they leave earth at a very young age. You see this as awful... however, if you were to look for the good in this judgment call, you might see it more as someone who left the costume party early... no more, no less.

If you find yourself judging war games harshly, you might see it as a group of souls who came into this lifetime to act out this game of war. They are here to play a role that they find interesting. Maybe they were a group of ministers in a past life and found religion stifling. So, this lifetime they chose to come to this dimension of fun and games and act out a whole new side of the equation.

Look, I know this is difficult for you to swallow, but it is true. You have come here again and again, and you continue with this game of incarnation. You come and you go quite often and you don't even *realize* how you are all connected, so how can you possibly *realize* how there is nothing wrong with playing these games.

The soul is allowed to enter this realm and don a costume and act out any role it chooses. You consciously know this *before* you enter. You see many choices available for each role, and you select ahead of time which role (with its various choices) best suits your needs. And just what are your needs? They are as wide and varied and diverse as each individual soul who comes here.

So, please begin to allow for everything to be okay as is. Once you begin to see how divinely perfect this world is, you will be accepting this world. Once you *accept* this world you will literally be loving this world. Why? Simply because acceptance is the gateway to love. Acceptance is embracing and embracing is hugging. Give the world a great big hug by *allowing* everything to be okay... no good versus bad... no right versus wrong... simply everything in perfect balance and harmony. Do not push life and the world away as unacceptable. You will become disillusioned with life and with the people around you. If you want to feel love, feel your own love of self, of life, of others. Let go of criticism. It is blocking your love source.

*T*he more you let go of your *need* to criticize, the happier you will become. You are not only the one who controls how happy you will be in your life; you are also the one who controls how sad you will become.

You may choose to look for the good in absolutely everything or you may choose to look for the bad. An easy way to tell which direction you are headed is by listening to yourself when you speak. Do you speak of happy, positive, fun things or do you speak of tragedy and unacceptable things? Do you have a good sense of humor about yourself or are you quite touchy about any comments made in jest? If you are quite touchy, you have a wound in you that requires healing. You may require the kind of healing that is thought of on earth as psychological. You may require coming into balance with your own energy.

If you contain a large psychological wound, you will be happy to know that it is always possible to let go of any damaging energy that you carry. You will find it quite necessary to let go of old wounds in order to heal and raise yourself up to a high level of joy and happiness. Once you let go of your wound, you will more than likely *feel* it for a short time as it rises up *in* you in order to leave you.

As old wounds surface, you will feel uncomfortable before you feel the good results of your release of a wound. Often you do not *realize* that the hurt and upset you are feeling is directly connected to some form of emotional or physical pain that you may have suffered in your past, or even in a past life.

So, as you stop to listen to yourself and how you may or may not criticize, you will find that you have a sore spot or touchy spot in your psyche. This spot is like a thorn that is tender to the touch. If anyone touches your tender wound, you blow up in anger and frustration. You begin to put them down simply because you are feeling pain.

Here is the tricky part: sometimes you misperceive what is being said to you, and you blow it all out of proportion and you make a mountain out of a molehill. This is due to the fact that, over the years, you have become most protective of your sore spot or your covered-up-by-you wound.

As you continue to cover your wound and protect it, you may find yourself snapping back at people and not trusting people and feeling a little standoffish. This is due to the fact that you have pain "in" you and you are trying to soothe this pain and keep you safe. Often this state of overprotection causes people to become aggressive in their efforts to keep people from touching their overly protected tender spot or wound. Sometimes those who are becoming overly protective feel that they must keep "everyone" from hurting them, and so they deem "everyone" a threat. If the wound is painful and inflamed, it may affect the individual to the point that he or she begins to fight for their own safety, by causing chaos and pain to self and to others.

In certain cases where the wound is very tender to the touch, the least little thing or even comment will set this wounded person off; and they may try to push the one who is causing their "perceived" pain away by threatening them or by killing them. After all, it started with a wound that was being touched by "perceived" danger. If one "thinks" he is in danger of being hurt further, he/she will protect themselves by getting rid of the "perceived" attacker; be the attacker real or perceived, does not really matter in an illusionary world.

You all have wounds; you all carry some sort of pain, be it emotional, or be it physical which is often caused by the emotions. You all strike back or lash out in some way. You may hit another physically or verbally, but the energy is all the same. Criticism starts the downslide into emotional revenge. Criticism is one of those energies that builds and compounds itself. Criticism leads to anger and resentment and rage and revenge, and then we have a gunman shooting up the town and claiming it was deserved.

It all starts with pain, and fear of being hurt further. Do not allow your pain and fear to rule you. You will follow criticism to anger, as that is the path it takes. Do not get on the criticism train if you want a happy life. It does not go to "happy town" or "happy life." Criticism leads somewhere you do not wish to go. It's not good or bad. It simply leads to somewhere you do not wish to go!

※

*A*s long as you continue to live from fear, you will not *feel* love. Love and fear are two opposing energies. Love lifts you up and fear lowers you. Love allows you to feel grateful and fear allows you to feel revengeful. When you are in a state of love, you are open and accepting. When you are in a state of fear, you are closed off and pushing back at life.

Fear allows you to push back and to fight back and to get all angry and fierce. Love allows you to open up and accept and *receive* in a very big way. Fear is not bad or wrong. Love is not bad or wrong. Allow everyone to make their own choices when it comes to fear and to love. If someone is ready and is asking for your advice on these two energies, I suggest you allow them to read this information. Do not push your perception of what is being said here onto another.

Your perception is just that... your perceived idea of what is being said. You all know how easy it is for you to misconstrue and misinterpret what is being said to you by someone else. You literally filter everything through *your* own personal consciousness which is made up of all that *you* contain including your fear and/or your love. You do not necessarily hear what is being said so much as you "color" everything that is being said through your use of judgment, criticism and personal intent. Intention is often what drives your motivation to change and "correct" situations and people in your lives. Sometimes your intentions are misdirected by fear and pain and eventually revenge.

You are a multi-dimensional being and you carry many layers of experience from both past life and this current life. Oh, did I say both? I really meant to say... you also have parallel lives and current "lives" that you are dealing with. Then we have the parts of you that are fragmented and disconnected from you, and, well you see how you are so much more than you currently see. There are so many hidden parts of you that you are unaware of; and I am simply trying to get you to "wake up" to just a small portion of your behavior, so that you might begin to *realize* how you act-out in response to all the many layers of beliefs and ideas and thoughts that you carry.

Until we get you to recognize who you are and how you operate the way that you do, I would like you to just *relax* and let go of telling everyone else how to live and what is right for them.

You are an unconscious human being trying to control your life out of "fear of life on earth." I will teach you how to be unafraid if you will just calm down and breathe. Please stop all the pushing and pulling of energy. You are tying *you* up in knots!

⚜

As you continue along your journey of discovery, I wish you to know that you are watched over and you are guided and you are loved more than you can ever imagine. You are cared for and cared about and you are considered innocent. You are perfect love and divine light, and you decided to take a trip into the unknown to express your divine light and consciousness *in* the unknown. Now you sit here and you wonder who you are and why you are here.

You are here as a divine expression of God. God is playing in matter and you are the part of God that decided to take on the role of explorer. You volunteered. All those billions of you volunteered to go into matter and see how you could affect matter. You each came with your own purpose or plan. Some don't really have a purpose beyond the fact that this adventure was open and available. It is similar to going to the beach and jumping in the ocean to see if you can catch a wave and ride it. For some of you it is simply "fun." For others it is a promise they made after leaving a previous lifetime. Some came because friends invited them to join with them. Others came to see if they could bring in a higher level of consciousness than they brought last time around.

Some of you even came in just to sit back and watch the show and be entertained. You all have a reason for being here and your reasons are as varied and different as you all are. So, how can you possibly know what is best for someone else if you do not know why they come to this earth playground?

You are all simply spirit children playing in matter. Lighten up please! Begin to enjoy your journey into the denser realm of matter. If you cannot enjoy it then I humbly remind you that you are putting out dense energy by your lack of joy, and your lack of gratitude, and your lack of appreciation, and your lack of acceptance.

You do not get to pick and choose here. The energies that bring you down out of awareness are the denser energies. That's just how it is on earth within matter. Dense energy sinks and pulls you down. Light energy lifts and pulls you up. If you can always focus on this fact, you will always be in control of your direction in this three-dimensional world. Dense equals down and light equals up. No good or bad; no right or wrong. Up or down is your choice.

Now, you may choose to stop your downward spiral by simply letting go of judgment and becoming an "observer." A person who becomes the observer does not get involved in the fray. A person who becomes the observer is not moving up or down, but is simply hovering at a specific level. You may choose to become the observer of your own personal life and of the life of others. It is okay to not get involved and to simply watch to see what the outcome will be.

You are all so programmed on earth to get involved, and to sometimes force yourself and others to do things you do not particularly want to do. Often manipulators will guilt the weaker among you into moving in one direction or another. This is common among family members and even in society. It is okay to not get involved in all the drama, and it is okay to simply sit back and *observe* how everyone is playing and acting-out on planet earth. If you are meant to be involved, you will not need to be talked into it. You will be on the forefront and you will *know* strongly that you are in your right place.

To listen to others is fine. To be manipulated and controlled may not get you where you wish to be.

So, as you go through your day today, I would like you to enjoy everything you do. Take your time and be patient with yourself. Know that you are loved more than you can ever imagine and know that you are watched over. You need not do anything to be loved. You simply are loved and accepted exactly as you are regardless of your choices. You are doing exactly what you came here to do. You are experiencing matter. You are expressing in this dense three-dimensional world. Have some fun with it. Allow it to be a good time and you will feel a little less stressed.

Be you! Love you! Enjoy being you... a divine, individual, one-of-a-kind chip off the force that is God. You are great indeed!

You will begin to discover a whole new way in which to live your life on earth. You will find that your creative energy is your greatest gift! You have been a part of God since the beginning. "The beginning of what?" – you ask. The beginning of time....

You are here on earth to seek out your true identity while in a state of unconsciousness – what a wonderful game that you play with yourself. You are part of everything and yet you do not *see* that you are. You communicate with everything and yet you do not know that you do. You are unconscious and this state of not knowing is the root of all your problems. You blame God and you blame those who have chosen to visit this earth with you; and you do not realize that this is all your choice and your desire and your gift.

So, how do we get you to wake up to the fact

that you are the sons and daughters of God, come to earth to play and bring in a little light energy? We might begin by gently nudging you now and then with the truth. We might also allow you to wake up on your own. Either way is simply a choice and either way is acceptable. If you have friends who have chosen to continue to stay unconscious and unaware, this is their choice. Free will allows you each to play this game however you choose. You are *not* in charge of their choices.

So, as we move along in this little unconsciousness game that you gods play, I wish you to remember that you have an identity that you don't even remember, so how can *you* tell *them* what to do or how to behave? Did you know that *you* make agreements with them before you enter earth? Did you know that before you enter earth, you are aware of the fact that you are a spirit, a soul, a part of God and that you are each eternal? Did you know that these gods that you all are, love to play act? And did you know that these gods that you are do not die ever; so they set up games where they might *pretend* that they do?

And did you know that when these gods set up their agreements to act out roles, they often take turns out of kindness? One god may ask another god/soul/spirit to shoot him or cause trauma to him in this earth game in order to *experience* this event. It is the same as you see in your movies. Sometimes the actor plays a comedic role. Other times the actor gets to play a more challenging dramatic role. It's all just fun and games on the spirit level, but because you are asleep and unaware that it is *not real* you get all upset and depressed, and you want revenge for any and all infractions.

Please let go of your belief that you die! You do not end – not ever. They do not end – not ever! Life does not end ever! Life changes and goes on to something else. There is no evil going on here! There is a game being played by gods who have forgotten who they are....

---

*Y*ou will soon discover how you have fooled yourselves and you will begin to allow life on earth to be a gift that is much loved. As you discover your own path to enlightenment, you will begin to let up on your harsher judgments regarding life and death.

You have spent a good deal of time putting yourselves down and putting others down. Now you are about to learn the *value* in lifting yourselves and your fellow man "up." You cannot do this as you talk about and criticize others. You will learn the gift of civility. Civility is an old term on earth that has lost its meaning. To be civil is to understand that you treat others as *you* would wish to be treated.

Many of you carry so much pain and confusion that you constantly talk about others in a very disrespectful manner. This is not bad or wrong. This simply will not raise your vibration, it will lower you a notch or two.

So, if you wish to continue your "rise up," I highly suggest you jump on the civility train and ride it right up to the gratitude train. These two rides are most important in your search for unconditional love. You actually *are* unconditional love that has lost its signal. You went haywire and now it is time to switch back from fear to love. You are *love*. You are meant to be accepting and flexible. You simply lost your ability to accept unconditionally and you "fell" into fear. Now we are going to pull you up out of fear and *allow* you to be all that you can be.

Fear has been in control on earth for eons, and now it is time to give love a chance to return. I would like to see you all happy and in love with yourselves. When you are happy and in love with yourself, you do not feel the need to judge or criticize. You become calm and peaceful and you do not jump to fearful conclusions with little provocation. Right now you are so fearful that you are defensive and you are overly protective of your wounds. I must get you to calm down and stop lashing out in order to get you to the next level which is peace.

I would like to see you all rise up at once; however that is not the plan. The plan is for you to rise up in groups. Once you have risen to a level of awareness that is helpful to others, you will be allowed to assist others as they make their efforts to rise up. How do you assist others in their rise? You ask them to stay calm and to hope for a good and positive outcome. You ask them to see the bigger picture, and to know that we are all connected, and we are only as strong and as aware as we allow ourselves to be.

If you have assisted someone and they do not agree with your view, then I suggest you allow them their own view. Once you wake up and see the bigger picture, your only job is to stabilize your position so you do not slip back into fear. If you do slip back, you at least will remember how to bring yourself back up to acceptance and love. As you assist others, you will find that it is not necessary to preach nor is it necessary to teach them anything. You simply *allow* them to share their truth with you and this will be the same as you allowing them to tell you about their viewpoint and what they are seeing.

Here is a little secret about energy: "What you resist *will* persist!" If you do not wish to see something do not fight against it or it will grow! Oh boy – that explains a lot about your situation on earth at this time, doesn't it? You are taught to stand up and fight for your rights and that this is the best course of action. However, you have forgotten how energy works. Fear creates more fear and love creates more love. What you put out comes back to its sender. You are creating *your* personal reality by the energy that you put into it day and night. Are you putting love and acceptance out into the universe to come back to you, or are you putting fear and anger out into the universe day and night to come back to you?

The choice is yours! It always has been and always will be....

※

You will begin to realize not everything is as you have been told. You do not truly understand creation and how spirit works.

As you continue to open up to new ideas, you will begin to see how everything is changeable and fixable and even undoable. You are living in a flexible field of matter; and this matter that you live in is capable of shape-shifting. You have not developed your abilities to the extent that you can shape-shift at this time in your evolution. You, however, have these capabilities.

As you learn who you are, you will also be

learning how you change. Most of what you know is considered quite basic in nature. As you develop your creative abilities you will see how you are capable of much more than you realize. You are also capable of hiding huge parts of *you* from yourself. One of these parts is your energy light being. You hide this part from yourself and you do not allow it to come forward and play an active role in your life.

Now – at the start of this book I told you how you do not leave your body at death and go out into the ethers somewhere. What I did not mention is how you do leave this material form and you go within to the entirety of yourself. The entirety of yourself is God force. You literally float within this vast creative force that is God, and there is no getting *out* of God, as God is "all there is." So, as you float *in* God, you also create *within* God. You build and live and thrive inside of God. You are literally the cells and atoms that make up God.

So, when you die, you do not leave and go somewhere else. There is nowhere else to go. You are part of God *and* you are a *projection* of God into matter.

So, let's discuss matter… you as God, enter matter by will. You literally *choose* to enter matter. It's like a small child who thinks it would be fun to jump into a movie screen and become one of the characters. So you jump in and begin your role within this movie called "Life on Earth." You then take over and begin to create within your movie. Each of you make individual choices as to what you will become as you grow in your role *within* your movie that you have selected for you.

Then you begin to act as if you are this character by using your personality to shape-shift and *become* this character. Once the life of this character has accomplished what it intended to accomplish it then *decides* on how to exit its role from the chosen movie.

Now, here is the catch... since you are God, you may choose to focus on multiple roles at one time. God has the ability to send out as many projections of himself/herself/itself as wished for to play this game of Life on Earth. So, basically, you are simply a projection of God force that has entered this material plane for the fun of it. Once you are *in* the movie you may continue to project and create projections (parts of you) of your own. You are always sending out energy, and then reading or translating that energy into meaning for *you* when the projections come back to you. All energy returns to its sender, so all parts of *you* eventually return to you.

So, when you die, you do not really leave your body and go out there somewhere. All energy returns to its sender and the original sender in this case (and in all cases) is God. So you go back to the field of God force that is creative energy and you continue to create and to project. You *feel* like you leave your body, but you simply remove your focus and energy and become an expanded version of yourself.

Your energy and your *connection* to God are all within the projected image of you. You go within to greater expanded awareness and you continue to move *within* the God force and create *within* the God force. Earth is simply a projection that lies within the God force. Everything is alive and available *within* God. You project many realities and many possibilities and personalities and so, so much more.

You are so incredibly vast and great and powerful, and you have no idea that you are. You put on the costume and now you truly *believe* that you are this insignificant little character, and your *belief* is what is creating this particular projected reality for you. Choose again! Choose to *believe* that absolutely everything is great just the way it is and you will be projecting a reality that is great!

So, now you think you may have made a big mistake coming into this material plane of matter and emotions. You really do belong wherever you wish to be, doing exactly what you wish to be doing. You are God and you *create*. Create what you wish whenever you wish. You are the children of God and you are simply playing and expressing your creativity.

It is not wrong for you to come into this earth plane and flex your creative muscles. You are energy that is moving and expanding and even growing in awareness. You are a spirit that has decided to enter matter to express within matter. You do nothing wrong! You are innocent and free of judgment in the eyes of God. You do not displease me and you do not offend me.

So, as you continue with your life on earth, I would like to see you a little more joyful and a little less sad. I would like you to express joy and contentment at the fact that you made it *in* to this dimension. Sometimes a soul waits for eternity to get the opportunity to enter physical life on earth. Some of you have come to earth many, many times and for others it is their first time.

Do not be afraid of life on earth. Enjoy life on earth. You obviously *chose* to be here, so why not *observe* your situation a little more thoughtfully until you know why you made this particular choice. Once you know why you *decided* to come to earth and experience physical life, you will be more conscious of your soul's/spirit's *intent*.

So, this is your lesson for today. I would like

you to sit and contemplate why your soul decided to enter this physical body. Was your spirit (you) excited to come back to earth? Were you (spirit you) sad to come and felt you needed to finish something? Were you (spirit you) asked to come to earth? Did you (spirit you) come with a group of friends simply because you did not wish to enter matter alone?

How did you decide on this choice? Were you told by a trusted guide or teacher that this would be a good experience for you? Did you want to be a physical being so that you might experience nature and the wind blowing gently through your hair? Did you want to experience watching a sunset through human eyes? Did you wish to get a glimpse of a beautiful colored rainbow? Or maybe you just wanted to be able to watch a butterfly flit by in front of you?

Did you want to experience childhood in a physical body? Or maybe you wanted to experience the joy and ecstasy of making love in physical form? Were you tired of looking in from the outside, so maybe you decided to dive right in – much like diving into the ocean rather than simply standing on the shore observing from outside and wondering what went on inside that ocean?

You are here on earth because you wanted to come here. Call me crazy, but I imagine that you did not come to be unhappy and disgusted with life. Please lighten up a little and begin to enjoy your choice. You will leave at some point and return to the field of all possibilities, and chances are you may choose earth again. You like life on earth and that is why you choose it so often. You may as well begin to see it as fun and lighthearted instead of fearful and dangerous.

Remember – *you are a creative being and you decide how to perceive absolutely everything!*

⁂

As you continue to live your life on earth, I would like you to realize that you are here because you have *chosen* this opportunity or experience. You did not get forced into it unless you agreed to come to earth under peer pressure. Sometimes a group of souls decide what is the best time to enter a body and they all work on the project together. Sometimes you ask for help and guidance in your decision and it is given. You are never told that you have to go unless you have asked to be told to go. It's much like asking your friends to tell you that you must go to the gym and workout.

So, if you have *decided* to be here in physical life, I want you to *enjoy* the ride. The easiest way to enjoy the ride, and all that life on earth offers, is to float until you can swim. If you are tossed into a river and cannot swim because you have not been taught to swim, a wise move would be to float. If you can float you can stay above the water and breathe. If you float you need to stay calm and breathe.

"Stay calm and breathe"- this is my advice to you. You are a spirit being who is learning to swim in this physical plane of dense energy. If you float you can stay above the fray. If you try to fight the water (energy) you create waves and turbulence in the water (energy). These waves affect you and they affect those around you. Stay calm please. Simply catch yourself when you are stirring the energy and sit down and breathe!

Once you have learned to float and to work *with* the energy in this way, you will be able to gently move yourself in the direction you wish to go, by simply moving your arms slowly and gently to avoid splashing. You are then moving *with* the energy without disturbing the energy. Next you may choose to submerge yourself and swim. This is done in a gentle, smooth fashion so as to avoid disturbances.

It is always up to you whether or not you make smooth transitions in life. These transitions are a daily part of life on earth, simply because life on earth is constantly shifting and changing and ebbing and flowing. You may fight the current and get upset about your *choice* to be here and experience this particular dimension, or you may learn to accept it and to enjoy the experience.

Remember – you are the one who decides what is awful and what is wonderful. For one person, being chased by a tiger through the jungle may turn out to be the most exciting experience of his life, which he will remember as a big "Wow! I did that!" For another person that experience may bring them to their knees emotionally. Such an experience may cause them to be extremely fearful the rest of their lives. It is all in how you *respond* to your experiences and you may decide to see absolutely everything differently. If you do so, you will be changing your entire life experience.

So, find something positive in each and every experience. Even the tiniest seed of positivity can turn to "gratitude," which can lift you up a little higher in the wave of energy that you are riding. Remember – the higher you go, the "lighter" you get. The "lighter" you get, the higher you can go!

So, think high, stay high and live high. Soon you will see how you are God, creating absolutely everything that you see by how you perceive it and how you respond to it!

*T*he next time you want to criticize or judge another, I would like you to remember that you are made up of energy. The energy that makes you up literally runs through every cell and every atom of your body. If you choose to criticize and to judge, you are sending a message to "criticize and judge" through your own body. You are literally telling your body to put you down a notch or two by your criticism.

What happens when you criticize? You want to put the person *down* that you are criticizing. This is how you can tell the difference between "judgment" and "calling something what it is." You know the difference in your tone when you speak. You feel the difference in your body when you criticize. You get all riled up, and sometimes sanctimonious, when you want to put someone or something *down*. You even put down ideas and people's hopes and dreams if they do not agree with your own.

When you run this energy put-down through your body, you are putting you down. So, as I have said repeatedly in this and other books, I would like to see you all take a break from judgment and simply relax and enjoy life. "How can I enjoy life with this awful, terrible situation going on" – you shout! You can sit down and shut up and breathe! Unless you are in a position of authority and can make positive changes to the situation, do not get involved in it.

Now I've done it! I have actually come right

out and said, "Do not get involved!" The reason I say this is simple. You are all so riled up and exhausted from being in a constant state of tension that I may never get through to you.

Look – you went to earth with the intent of creating something godlike. You got involved in your role as a bad guy or a good guy and so now you think you are the character that you play. Take off your costume! The light being that is *in* you is also in that guy that you hate. The light being that is in you is part of everything. The light being that is *in* you *is* God force! The light being that is in you is simply projecting an imagined scenario, and then jumping in to live within its own projected scenario.

Do not be so upset with the roles that you are playing. This is a dream within a dream. This is not real and you are not really human. You are a light being acting out a role, and you forgot that you are simply in a costume (body) and playacting. You are *all* God's children and you have entered this reality to play – much like a child who goes out to the backyard to play cops and robbers or cowboys and Indians. You *chose* your role! You decided to be the good guy this time because you got to be the bad guy last time. Your light being friends allowed you to play the good guy and now they are playing the bad guy just as *you* asked them to.

Now it is time to take a break from your roles

and rest for a while. God has been watching over you as you play this game of "Life on Earth," and God has decided that you are getting a little too carried away with your roles. It's time to calm down and breathe. It may even be time for a nap….

---

*F*rom the beginning you have been a light being. You have always been light and you will always be light. From time to time, you choose to don a costume and look like something other than what you are. This is common and a fun thing to do in the world of spirit.

Once in a while you even break out in dance and song. The easiest way to dance (if you are a light being) is to take on a form with legs and arms. Of course, you may choose to *imagine* that you have arms and legs but it is not quite the same, or as much fun as actually taking on matter and growing arms and legs.

You will find that for a light being to enter matter, the light being must take certain steps to assure success. Once in matter, the light being soon forgets how it chose to take on form in order to participate in this particular dimension. Now; once you have taken on form, you may begin to grow as a human and you are then subjected to human laws. You however, know that you are a light being and you find human laws quite limiting and often quite grotesque.

These laws are often forced upon you by society and by the energy that permeates this particular dimension. Some of the laws have been created to protect humans from a barbaric society. Humans have emotions and they have a mind. The mind within the human body has been formed by eons of struggle and fighting for survival. Humans don't realize that there really is no death and so they struggle to protect themselves from death. Once a human becomes *aware*, on a conscious level, that death does not exist, that human can begin to live in a state of grace. She will no longer *feel* the *need* to lash out to protect herself. She will no longer *feel* the urge to save herself at all costs.

Once the human really realizes the eternity of his being, he will begin to "lighten up" in a whole new way. He will *know* that it is not necessary to *fear* any outcome as he will begin to *see* how everything is changing and vibrating and moving just as it is meant to in this material world. You are not here to suffer; however, you may *allow* suffering to occur by how you perceive what is going on here.

You are a light being and you are creating without knowing that you are. You are sending out a specific vibration that is affecting how your brain *views* and *perceives* reality in this dimension. The more fear you carry regarding life on earth, the greater difficulty you will have *accepting* life on earth, or life in physical form. The more disconnected you become from your source of light, the greater your level of difficulty in operating within the human form within the world of matter.

The greatest gift you can give yourself is to wake up to your own beliefs and fears, and turn your beliefs and fears into love and acceptance. This will allow you to rise *above* all the fighting and arguing and war. *Raise you up!* Do not push at everyone else to see it your way. If someone is ready to *hear* that love and acceptance are the answer, you may share that bit of wisdom; however, please do not browbeat people with your wisdom. Sharing is one thing, pushing-at is another. You really do know when you are *pushing* your agenda on another versus when you are simply sharing a secret little insight like, "Everything is really in divine order and progressing just as planned."

So, sit back and relax and allow the "light being" in you to *express* itself, and to sing and dance and shine its love on this world.

*Y*ou are probably feeling quite confused by now. This information that I send to you through Liane is quite controversial and quite different from what you are normally told.

Think of yourself as an animal that has gotten tangled up in barbed wire. You are frightened and kicking and screaming and moaning in pain. I am here to rescue you from yourself. I am here to tell you to stop kicking and fighting. Your best course of action at this juncture is to stay calm and allow something higher than yourself to take charge. The barbed wire represents the energy you have entangled yourself in. You are so twisted up in your fear and revenge thoughts, that you are tightening the wire that surrounds you by putting out more of these barbed lines of energy to surround you.

Sit down and relax please! I do not wish to see you create further stress and strain for yourself and others. Stress and strain cause tension. Tension causes anger and anger leads to greater tension and eventually to fighting. Fights start small and grow to include your friends and family. Division increases until this fight turns to mobs that are angry, and then entire neighborhoods, and then entire countries who do not know the whole story or even why they are fighting.

Humans fight out of fear and out of defense. You are not being chased or shot at now – are you? I am assuming that you are sitting somewhere where you can read this material. If you are not, at this moment, being chased or threatened then I highly suggest you "allow" your thoughts to calm down and come to a loving space. Any "perceived" threat or danger is not *in this moment*. It is in the future "what if" that you are presently creating – "What if this happens?" "What if that happens?"

Stay in this present moment and "do not," I repeat "do not" project yourself into a negative future projection. You are God! You create! Stop creating versions of reality that you do not want! Begin to project positive versions forward and *you* will be assisting humanity in a very big way. I know this may be challenging for you, and I "see" how this planet is surrounded by all the fear energy that the unconscious gods of this planet have projected. If I can just get enough of you earth gods to switch from fear to love we will begin to "see" results. We will begin to see the awakening of humanity. We will begin to see your true self which is light! You are the light of this world – begin to act like it!

※

*Y*ou will begin to discover a new way of viewing life on earth once you have turned your fear energy to love (acceptance) energy.

You are so concerned with future "what ifs" that you spend a good deal of your time being concerned about these "what ifs." You are no longer living in the present moment and have projected your energy into these future possibilities. If you are going to continue to *project* into future possibilities, I would suggest you make these possibilities positive. Do not fret and do not worry. Use your energy to calm yourself and to move towards a positive outcome in all situations. This is using your "power to create" in a more helpful-to-you manner.

Now, as far as death and destruction are concerned, I do believe that the majority of you who are currently reading this are safe and sound at this very moment. Focus on that! Focus on this very moment and learn to live in the "now." You will find that it is much more comfortable and uplifting to live in this present moment.

You are here on earth to experience life on earth. You made it in! You went through the birth process or you entered your body after the birth process and you survived. You were able to merge your vibration with that of matter, and you (the light being you) were able to achieve entry into this world of illusion and wonder and physical senses. Aren't you happy that you achieved your goal? You went unconscious and became totally unaware of who you are and your connection to God. That in itself is quite a feat.

Now you are in matter and you are unconscious and I am here telling you that it is time to wake up and *remember* that you are a light being and you are part of God.

You actually are part of God and you actually do create. I will continue to tell you this until you *realize* and begin to "feel" it. You are here to experience all that you chose to come here to experience. Get on with it and become all that you wished to be by *allowing* yourself to shed some light on all situations that may occur.

Always see everything in the best possible light. Always give the benefit of doubt as to anyone's guilt. Always look for the good in absolutely every situation.

You are moving on and you are carrying God right inside of you. You are never, ever alone. You are watched over and loved and you are never bad or wrong… not ever.

You are the light that has come into matter to play and experience within this dimension. Have fun with it! Enjoy your time here! Soon enough you will decide to return to your true identity and many of you will miss this playground and return again and again for more fun and games….

❦

*F*or the most part, you are moving right along in your evolution as planned. Soon you will rise above your current state of awareness and you will understand how you are put together. You have available to you many techniques to assist you in your rise in consciousness.

Most of you do not consider yourselves to be light beings. You are so connected to the human side that you go unconscious and act-out quite easily. As you grow in awareness, this will change and you will be less activated by fear, and more calm due to awareness.

This is your path. This is the path of all light beings who descend into matter. It is a tight fit and sometimes uncomfortable for the light beings to stay "in" body. You might think of it as trying to capture "light" in a bottle. It is quite an achievement.

So, now you are "in" matter and you are beginning to wake up to the fact that you are. This will lead you to the awareness that not all parts of you are "in." After all, how can you capture "all light" in one little bottle? So, much of you is left out of this particular body and is off on other adventures – some right here on earth, others on other planets and dimensions.

You will find that you are not located in one place at any given time. You are like a focus that *shifts* from place to place. You are here one minute and over there the next. Now, here is the interesting part. There really is no "over there." There is only the "here and now" that you are focusing on. Think of your television or computer device. You may go from one channel to the next with simply the push of a button. You may go from one life to the next by simply changing channels. You may focus on any movie you wish and it is all up to you. You may *choose* a comedy or a drama. You may decide to turn off your TV or computer and not "focus" on drama or comedy. You may decide to go within and just breathe.

All life is but a movie and "you" are the projector of said movie. You may change the movie by projecting something new. I would encourage you to begin to project peace and calm and love. These energies will assist you as you return to your source, which is the light of awareness. Your source, the light, has always been and will continue to "be." You may access your source, the light, anytime from anywhere. You are divine light in a bottle and you have forgotten your source. You will wake up and you will remember. You will begin to "feel" that you are so much more than your accomplishments here on earth. You will begin to "know" that there is so much more than life in a bottle. You will begin to rise up and see how you are so expansive that you are capable of seeing beyond this bottle.

Life on earth is not always what you thought it might be, but you did choose to enter a bottle and experience separation. You know that you are really part of everyone and everything and they are part of you. You are all in disguise. Your arms and legs and toes and fingers may be wearing a different color than you, but they are still part of your body. Do not hate your parts simply because they are a different color or because they do not act like you think they should. You are hating "you." Stop all hatred, as all hatred is self-hatred.

When you begin to accept all parts of you, you will be allowing you to become a whole being once again. Once separation ends, you will become all that you can be, which is a source of light right here inside of matter.

As we begin our rise up out of an unconscious state, we will see a little conflict appear in our world. This conflict will be the reflection of the conflict, or struggle, that is going on with each individual who is rising up and waking up. You do not create energy disturbances and not feel or experience them in some way.

Now, as you rise you begin to slough off or let go of the denser beliefs and notions that you have always lived by. You may become frustrated by the pull of energy *within* you. When you have a strong pull from dense energy that has been rooted in your belief system for a very long time, you may feel quite conflicted and even act-out a bit. This conflict *within* you is to be expected. You may feel good and positive one day and revert downwards to less positive feelings the next. This will eventually pass and you – your energy – will come into balance.

As you become less and less frustrated with this process, the struggle will become less and less and you will eventually level out in a more positive state of mind. This is your goal. Your goal is to move from negative energy to positive energy. Why? Simply because negative energy is dense and pulls you down, while positive energy is light and lifts you up.

So, as you continue to wake up and rise up, do not be concerned by those moments when the struggle to stay positive is a little too much for you. At those times when you want to come out yelling and screaming that "everything is awful," I want you to take a deep breath and find just one thing in your life that is wonderful. That one thing might be a circumstance, or a family member, or a friend, or a plant in your yard. That one wonderful thing may be a pet, or a painting, or your favorite song, or your favorite flower. That one wonderful thing may be your gift of vision, or your gift of hearing. That one wonderful thing may be your ability to take on light, and to shine your light on and in this world.

Focus on this one wonderful thing until you become calm, and then write the word "love" over and over again until you no longer feel like yelling at the world. Energy follows "thought" and your energy (you) goes where ever you send it. Do not send all of your energy out into a situation or event that you do not wish to be married to. Do not entangle your energy (you) anymore than it (you) is already entangled. The more entangled you become the more difficult it becomes for you to rise "up" to the next stage of awareness.

I know it is difficult to stay positive when you are bombarded by negativity, but *you* can do this! You can and will rise above your current level of frustration and struggle and fear. You *will* rise up to love and light and pure consciousness. There is a saying, "It is always darkest before the dawn." Know that the dawn of a new way of seeing yourself and your world is on its way....

*T*he one and only thing you need to concern yourself with is joy. Are you joyful? If you do not experience joy, you are losing out on a big opportunity.

Now, when I speak of joy, I do not mean "happiness no matter what." Joy is more a feeling of pleasure and contentment. Being content has become much underrated on earth. You all rush here and rush there to accomplish your dreams, and you are exhausted and worn down. If you could simply live and let live, you would feel a little more contentment in your life. You are so programmed by society to become an achiever of success that you constantly "push" at yourself to do more and be more.

With many of you, acceptance is a word that denotes loss and giving up and giving in. It is not acceptable to just "be." It is not enough to be alive and well. If you were to tell your friends that you are well and content, they would not understand that you are in a very good place. You will find that contentment brings you more of the same. You will find that joy brings you more of the same. You will also find that struggle and aggression bring you more of the same.

Set your path to contentment and watch your entire body relax. You do not have to be the best. You do not require accolades for your success, unless you "believe" that you do. You do not require riches, unless you "believe" that you do. Why do you think it is called "the treadmill of life?" Once you start chasing after your dreams, you will continue to set higher and higher goals with greater payoffs.

Now, don't get me wrong here... dreams are good and goals are good. I am simply pointing out how energy works in case you are ready to stop and get off your treadmill. It is all up to you and it is all simply a choice.

So today I would like you to look at your life and see if you are caught up in a cycle that is not bringing you joy or contentment. Let go of stress and struggle, and you will be allowing space for joy to enter your life. Live in the moment and be sure to show "tolerance" for those who are very different from you. You are moving "up" now, and when you move up you *allow* for new energy to enter your life pattern. Stay focused on joy and contentment, and use your gratitude to move you up the ladder of success.

You have been down for some time now and it is past time for waking up and rising up. You are the light of this world. You carry God – the creative force of the universe – right inside of you. You are the alpha and the omega. As you continue to rise, you will continue to calm down and relax and accept. Acceptance after all is love, and love is what you truly are.

You will find that you are at your best when you are calm and peaceful. You shine your brightest at that time and you "feel" your best. Do you want to feel good about yourself? Sit down and be at peace. End the struggle *within* and you will no longer be sending out energy that is conflicting. You will be sending out energy that is peaceful and calm. You control the projector, as you *are* the projector of the movie of your life on earth. You are like a computer that has a virus, and I am letting you know that you need to delete and erase some negative energy in order for your computer to function properly.

You may choose not to listen and you may think that you know best. This too is okay. Everything is actually okay and moving along quite nicely. So, why do I bother to write this to you and through Liane? You are all screaming for "help," so I am doing what I can to assure you that you are safe and have never been in any danger, simply because you are an infinite light being!

※

The most important thing to remember is "love." Love is the highest energy vibration and love will always return you to yourself. You are a love light and you are part of the greatest love of all.

Most of you do not *realize* how often you give your energy, your power, over to fear. Fear will not assist you in your goal unless your goal is to be burdened by dense energy.

As you continue to move forward in this life that *you* have chosen, I wish you to remember that you are always going to be watched over and guided, and loved beyond your imagination. You are the light of this world and you are appreciated for the simple fact that you exist. You are not to be disrespected for your efforts to create a life in matter. You are so wonderful and yet you think you are so nothing and so unimportant. If you could just see you from a much higher perspective, you would see how awesome and wondrous you truly are.

You have come here to earth many times and yet you continue to forget that this is simply a game that you all play with yourselves. If you could all just calm down and breathe, we would see you move a slight bit closer to peace on earth and heaven brought down to earth.

As I stated at the start of this book, this information has been a gift to Liane. It is her personal guidance coming through to assist her in the next phase of her life on earth. I realize that you are all connected and you are actually all one, so this material may be of interest to you also. It all depends on where you are in your waking up process and how eager you may or may not be to move upward.

So, as you come to the end of this book, please know that you are always in control of your own personal reality. You may choose to end chaos by simply *seeing* it differently. You may choose to "focus" on whatever reality you decide to exist in. Please remember that absolutely everything, including you, is energy and this energy is affected by and *moved* by energy. You come into existence and you go out of existence. You focus here and you shift your focus to there. You are a sailor one moment and you are a housewife and mother the next.

Energy moves and energy creates greater waves of energy. Energy may vibrate and energy may oscillate. You are here one minute and back in the God force the next. You are in 1988 one minute and in 2088 the next. You are energy! You fluctuate and you oscillate from time frame to time frame. Remember – time does not really exist, so all time is in the now. You may be a caveman right now this moment, sitting by your fire. You are also this you sitting and reading this information. You are also God, the entire field of possibilities, who is writing this to you. You are *in* God and *in* your cave and sitting *here* right now this instant.

So, where is your focus? Who will you choose to be today? You literally oscillate like a blinking star. Your light enters so many shapes and forms, and so many parallel realities and dimensions. How can you possibly judge this life on earth when you do not even realize who you and your fellow earth inhabitants are?

Now, I wish to end this book and give Liane a much-needed break. It is not always easy on her to channel information that is directly opposed to the thought energy that circles this planet. Her body is made up of all the denser thoughts and beliefs that are formed by society and personal experience. As I channel information through her it affects her cellular vibration, which in turn triggers the denser energies to "release" and move to the surface where they may be felt.

Sometimes the energies that bring you *down* are right inside of your own cells. All is not lost. You may always release any dense energy and rise *up* a little higher. You too may feel sluggish and confused as these denser energies leave you. This is known as clearing and releasing, and I have written extensively about it throughout my series of 20 Loving Light Books. If you feel the need to go within and clear out some old debris, you may be interested in reading this series.

For now I will leave you with this thought… You are but an energy light that is the thought and imagination of God. You are like an idea that has been sent forth from the divine….

God

Leaving My Body
by Liane

Years ago I had a minor operation. Everything went well until after surgery. Then, apparently someone inadvertently gave me a drug twice instead of just the single dose.

I went unconscious and the doctors and nurses were trying to revive me. I remember a doctor's voice yelling at me to "wake up," and at one point he even said "come back!" But the only thing I wanted to do was leave. I was aware of several voices around me in my hospital room and I remember thinking, "Why don't they all just go away and leave me alone!"

I was having so much fun and felt like I was leaving my body and moving up out of the top of my head. I felt so good and happy to be going wherever it was that I was going. I think the doctor may have injected me with something to reverse the drug. When I did open my eyes there were five or six doctors, nurses and attendants around my bed. Apparently it took them a while to bring me back.

I've never forgotten that feeling and how happy I was to be going out the top of my head, to where ever it was that I was going.

Sometimes I have little chats with God in my head, so today I asked about my experience and he/she said he would write the answer for me. This is what he wrote:

"When you leave your body at death, you may use a spiral method. This is where you feel like you are spiraling up out of the top of your head. Other options are available to you. You may simply pop out of your body or you may float up out of it.

Often times, people remember floating above their body as they leave and this exit is most common. Sometimes you simply turn off your earthly awareness and in the blink of an eye you are seeing an entirely new dimension, depending on how far you wish to go with your awareness. Not often, but sometimes, you actually wake up somewhere new. You wake up in a different place with a whole new way of interacting with that place.

There are unlimited dimensions as well as unlimited layers of reality. You may travel on a light beam or you may feel like you haven't moved, yet everything around you has changed.

When you leave your body it is a bit like leaving home. You may not know consciously where you are going, however, you do *know* that you are moving on energetically. As you continue to move on you may experience any multitude of feelings and vibrations. You are a light being and you move around within the vastness of your own beingness. You are on an inward journey and you have always been a light that is experiencing the many facets of its own self.

Once you exit your body you may focus on other parts of 'you,' or facets of 'you' that are in the various areas of your consciousness. Remember – consciousness is an inside job. You might think of death of the body as the end of a show on TV and you simply focus on the next show, and then the next, and so on – for all time. Why? Because you can, and because you enjoy the adventure!

Sometimes you even leave the body while it is still healthy. This is often the case with coma patients. You are out of body exploring and having a good ol' time, and sometimes you are out too long and the body is given up. This is often most difficult for family and friends, however, sometimes you as light beings agree to this type of an exit before you enter the earth and physical form.

So, there is an expansive variety of possibilities and an expansive variety of ways to leave this life on earth. You come and go often. You get involved in various scenarios from many different times in earth history. Not only do you get involved in many different times historically, you also project into more than one form in any one time in history. You also project into other forms in other dimensions. There are as many possibilities as there are grains of sand in the ocean.

So please, do not be afraid that you might end. There are so many you's that you will never discover all of you... not until 'you' decide to come back to the 'awareness' that you are indeed the entirety of *all that is!*"

Epilogue

Liane: God – are you light?

God: Yes.

Liane: What is the original purpose for life on earth or in the material plane?

God: It is to be able to transcend the gift of eternity. You wanted to break away from being infinite and at peace and tranquil and all-knowing. You wanted something different, unique, untried… "Let's go to a place where we don't know all the answers." "Let's take our consciousness to a whole different level." "Let's pretend like we are not God and infinite wisdom." "Let's start from the bottom and work our way up." "Let's pretend that we know absolutely nothing and try to see how far we can get without using our powers." "Let's pretend we're a baby who doesn't know how to walk and can't yet speak, just to see how it feels."

"Oh, I have a great idea – let's see who can get back to consciousness and Godhood first." "Let's see which techniques work the best to get us back to ourselves – our God-selves." "This will be a fun game and some of us can actually stay behind to guide and coach from here." "First one to go unconscious, enter the material plane and regain awareness while still *in* the material plane wins!"

"Yes – good idea, this sounds like fun." "Is everyone ready – let's go. First you must go unconscious then, once *in* matter, you must wake up." "This ought to keep us entertained for a while...."

God smiles as he watches his children at play....

The End!

Introduction to
The Loving Light Books Series

There are many ways to go within to your core or your heart center. When you reach deep within your own psyche you will enter the core of your being. This is where soul and spirit resides.

For those of you who wish to reconnect with your own God-self I highly suggest that you read and reread the "Loving Light Books" series. This series is designed to draw you "within" to your own God-self and to allow you to peel away the layers that prevent you from becoming the loving, radiant being that you truly are.

This series of 20 books was received by my pen (Liane) over a 10 year span of time and are quite remarkable. You will be led from an earthly way of viewing life to a more God-like way of viewing life. Everything is subjective in this three-dimensional world that you now call home. You, however, are a spiritual being and your life as a human is out of balance since you decided to enter matter. We will feed you information in this series that will allow you to *perceive* your current life in a whole new way.

These books were written for my channel and are most helpful to anyone who wishes to add more love and understanding to their life here on earth. If you are happy with where your life stands now, I do wish you well. If, on the other hand, you would like to learn more about your own spirit essence and how to connect with the part of you that draws love and unconditional light into your life, I highly suggest you begin your journey *within* by reading these helpful books.

    I wish you well on your journey to discovering "you"....

God

The Loving Light Books Series

Book 1: God Spoke through Me to Tell You to Speak to Him
Book 2 & 3: No One Will Listen to God & You are God
Book 4: The Sun and Beyond
Book 5: The Neverending Love of God
Book 6: The Survival of Love
Book 7: We All Go Together
Book 8: God's Imagination
Book 9: Forever God
Book 10: See the Light
Book 11: Your Life as God
Book 12: God Lives
Book 13: The Realization of Creation
Book 14: Illumination
Book 15: I Touched God
Book 16: I and God are One
Book 17: We All Walk Together
Book 18: Love Conquers All
Book 19: Come to the Light of Love
Book 20: The Grace is Ours

Also by Liane Rich
The Book of Love
For the Love of God: An Introduction to God
For the Love of Money: Creating Your Personal Reality
Your Individual Divinity: Existing in Parallel Realities
For the Love of Life on Earth
Your Return to the Light of Love: a guidebook to spiritual awakening

"Is it theoretically possible to *receive information* from a God process, since the universal God process is inside everything?"
Gary Schwartz, Ph.D. – The G.O.D. Experiments

God's Pen

I first heard the voice of God in 1988. I was sitting in my back yard reading a book when this big booming voice interrupted with, "I am God and I will not come to you by any other name." I felt like the voice was everywhere – inside of me as well as in the sky around me. I was so frightened that I ran in my bedroom to hide.

This was not the first time that I heard voices. I had been communicating with my own spirit guide or soul for about a year. I guess my depth of fear regarding God, and all that he represented to me at the time, was just too much.

I spent two days trying to avoid the voice of God, which was patiently waiting for me to respond. By the second day I was exhausted from lack of sleep and decided to give in and talk with him. This turned out to be the greatest gift and best decision of my life.

In the beginning the voice of God would wake me in the middle of the night and tell me it was time to write. He said I had promised to do this work (I assumed he was talking about the soul/spirit me). I would drag myself up to a sitting position and watch in amazement as my hand flew across the page, while I tried to keep up by reading what was being written.

It was always so much fun to wake up the next morning and grab my notebook to see what God had written during the night. After some time the voice stopped waking me and I became comfortable picking up my pen and writing for God first thing in the morning. I think in the beginning I had to be awakened while still semi-conscious from sleep so I wouldn't object too much to the information that was being channeled through me.

As I grew less and less afraid (and more trusting) of God, he was able to communicate greater information. Some of the information is quite controversial, but I felt it important to just let it be and not censor it. I present the writings in this book to you as they were given to me.

For privacy reasons I am using a pen name. I asked God for a good pen name and he guided me to Liane which (I was told) in Hebrew means "God has answered."

At one point I became a little concerned about my sanity in all this, so I went to a hypnotherapist to find out what I was doing. Under hypnosis I saw this incredibly huge beam of light with a voice coming from within it. It was a giant "loving light" and felt so comforting and kind. It felt like that's where I came from. After that I stopped worrying about my sanity. If this is crazy, I think it's a very good kind of crazy to be....

In loving light, *Liane*

Loving Light Books

Available at:
Loving Light Books: www.lovinglightbooks.com
Amazon: www.amazon.com
Barnes & Noble: www.barnesandnoble.com

Also on request at local bookstores

www.ingramcontent.com/pod-product-compliance
Lightning Source LLC
LaVergne TN
LVHW011420080426
835512LV00005B/174